# If He Is Raped

Alan McEvoy, Debbie Rollo,
and Jeff Brookings

# If He Is Raped

*A Guidebook for Parents,*
*Partners, Spouses, and Friends*

Alan McEvoy, Debbie Rollo,
and Jeff Brookings

Learning Publications, Inc.
Holmes Beach, Florida

ISBN 1-55691-150-5

**Learning Publications, Inc.**
5351 Gulf Drive
P.O. Box 1338
Holmes Beach, FL 34218-1338

Printing:  5  4  3  2  1      Year:  3  2  1  0  9

Printed in the United States of America

# Contents

# Acknowledgments

This book would not have been undertaken without the courage of people who were willing to talk about that which has remained for too long a dark secret . . . the same-sex rape of males. To those males who have survived sexual assault, and to their family and friends, this book is dedicated.

We are especially grateful for the insights of Michael Scarce, Alice Vachss, Shirley Foor, D. P. Hall, R. D. Bell, and Derek Williams. Special thanks also to Janet Clee, who saw the need for this book, to the volunteers and staff at Call Rape, Inc., for their encouragement, and for the unconditional support of G. L. and Bette Shealy and Sandy Boyce. We are likewise indebted to Vicki DiOrazio for the book design.

And thank you Edsel and Ruth Erickson for always cultivating the very best in others.

# 1
# Understanding the Basics

What if you learn that your son has been sexually molested, or that your husband suffered the pain and humiliation of forced anal penetration by several men when caught alone, or that a close male friend was forced to place another man's penis in his mouth or be shot? How would you react? What would you do to help him recover? Consider the following true story.

## "We Were His Friends"

*He thought that because we were his friends, we would understand. We were college roommates, teammates, and drinking buddies. We laughed together, poked fun at each other, and always found humor in one another's lives. So naturally, "Bugs" thought he could trust "the guys" with what had happened. After all, we were his closest pals.*

*Walking back to the apartment one night, Bugs took a shortcut through an alley. He was stopped by two armed men. Each brandished a knife and demanded money. Terrified, Bugs gave them his wallet. He offered no resistance. But then, one of the men put a knife to Bugs's throat and ordered him to remove his pants. They each penetrated him anally and ejaculated.*

*When Bugs stumbled his way into the apartment, he said noth-
ing. He showered and went to his room. None of us thought twice
about his behavior; it was late and it had been a long week. The
next day was Saturday; we had no classes. The guys were hanging
out, having a few beers and partying. As we socialized, Bugs remained silent and withdrawn. He was drinking more heavily than
the rest of us, but he often did that. As the alcohol took effect, I'm
sure each of us thought that everyone was having a grand time.*

*Out of the blue Bugs said, "I've got to tell you guys some-
thing." We listened in stunned silence. None of us had ever thought
about a man being raped by other men. No one knew what to say.
And in that moment of silence, the group's response was being for-
mulated. It could have gone either way. But it didn't. The alcohol,
the climate of mirth, and the ignorance of young men to know how
to respond to the emotional turmoil of a man who had been raped
set the stage for what happened next.*

*Because much of the "bond" that held us together was based
upon poking fun at one another, the first response to Bugs's account was a "humorous" remark. One of the guys said, "So Bugs,
did you get off?" That remark gave permission to the rest of us. A
cascade of jokes followed. We even debated whether his nickname
should be changed from "Bugs" to "Bugger Boy," or just plain
"Buggers."*

*I do not think that any of us meant to do harm. Rather, our in-
sensitivity was born of two things: ignorance about rape and its
consequences, and an established pattern of interaction that never
permitted any of us to be serious about things that were deeply
emotional.*

*Not long after that, Bugs moved out of the apartment. He
avoided us. We heard that he was drinking heavily and that he was
doing poorly in his classes. A woman we knew who had talked to
Bugs joined us one afternoon. She told us about being raped herself, and she described for us what she knew Bugs must be going*

2

*through. All of us felt ashamed. But by then, the damage had been done. Because of our insensitivity, we failed a friend . . . and we lost him.*

Rape can happen to anyone, including males. The way you respond to a male who is raped is extremely important because your reaction could make his life miserable far beyond the moment of the sexual offense. Depending upon what you say and do, you also could facilitate his recovery. Even if you do not know that a male close to you has been sexually assaulted, your unwitting references to sex or about what it means to "be a man" can help or hurt his recovery. Because you are important to his recovery, you need to know what to do and what not to do if a loved one, a friend, or even a male stranger, tells you that he has been raped.

The focus of this book is on males who are raped by other males. Although there are rare instances of female perpetrators and male victims, the vast majority of cases of male rape involve males assaulting other males. This book outlines the most important things one should say and do when confronted with an incidence of male rape. Conversely, we explain what one must avoid doing so as not to make the life of a loved one, a friend, or a stranger who has been sexually victimized more hurtful than it already is. In order to know what you should and should not do, however, it is critically important to understand the effect of male rape upon the victims. It also is important to consider the similarities and the unique implications of male rape as compared to female rape in this culture.

## Male Rape Victims

When you hear the word "rape," your mental image probably is that of a female victim and a male perpetrator. True enough, the majority of rapes involve female victims and male assailants. But there are exceptions. We know that a substantial number of rape victims* are male, though no one knows for certain how many. Recent estimates suggest that perhaps 5 percent or more of all forcible rapes involve male victims.** The lack of an accurate reporting system for male rape (including rapes in prison) and the reluctance of males to divulge their victimization, means that we will probably never know the full magnitude of the problem.

Because understanding the nature of rape is critical to your role in helping the victim, we want you to be clear about what happened to him. Rape is *not* about sex. Rape is about *power, control, and domination*. Rape is a *violent crime*. The victim of rape has not "asked for it" and does not "enjoy it." In the case of male rape, the victim has been *forced* to endure anal penetration, or *forced* to perform fellatio, or *forced* to touch another male's genitals. In the case of male rape, the victim often is terrorized with threats of extreme bodily harm or even death. Rape is life threatening and life altering. Rape severely traumatizes the victim. Knowing the nature of rape now, however distressing and shocking the words might be to you, will help you to gain the most benefit from this book.

Most of our knowledge about rape in general reflects studies of females who have been sexually assaulted. In recent years, we have learned much about how to help females regain their lives after a rape. To date, however, few studies have paid attention to the needs of males who are raped. Even so, we know that important similarities and differences exist between female and male rape victims. For example, for both males and females the experience of being sexually victimized is traumatic. In both cases, recovery from the

---

*Rape experts often use words such as "victim" or "survivor" to describe a person who has been sexually assaulted. Generally speaking, a "victim" is a person who suffers severe injury from another, and a "survivor" is a person who lives beyond a traumatic event. In this sense, the term "survivor" implies that a person has achieved a state of recovery from the trauma, whereas "victim" suggests that the person who has been harmed is still struggling to recover. A victim remains a victim until he or she decides to cease being a victim. This book attends to the needs of male victims on their way to becoming survivors.

**For more information on male rape, we highly recommend that you read *Male on Male Rape: The Hidden Toll of Stigma and Shame* by Michael Scarce, New York: Plenum, 1997.

assault is affected by the support, or lack of support, received from family and friends. And in both cases, the perpetrator is nearly always a *male*.

Yet, as we shall see, this last point is also the basis for understanding important differences between male and female victims of rape. For males, being raped by a person of the same sex has significant implications for how they:

- perceive their rape
- behave after the rape
- view their sexuality
- are judged by others
- recover from the assault.

Whether you are a parent, sibling, partner, friend, or advocate, there are practical ways to talk with and support the male victim. There are ways to positively aid him in what he thinks, how he behaves, and how he copes throughout his recovery. Your part in his recovery is important because the way in which you treat him after the assault can affect how he views you, himself, and the experience for the rest of his life. Your responses in the aftermath of the sexual assault can have a profound impact on your relationship with him. We encourage you to remain hopeful as you both work to smooth the bumpy road to recovery.

Because the stakes are so high, this book challenges you to *believe in the victim*. It encourages you to *normalize* his intense feelings, to *validate* his emotional and social concerns, and to *empower* him to accept and to cope with his attack without becoming totally consumed by it. As someone who cares about him, he needs to know that:

- you believe he is not permanently impaired by the violation

5

- you are optimistic about his recovery and his ability to put his life back in order
- he can overcome his wounds, even if the rape is never forgotten
- you believe he has the inner strength to resist the stigma and shame associated with being a male rape victim, and that you will help him in his efforts to resist
- he can achieve recovery by turning his anger into the motivation for regaining control over his life and moving forward, despite what has been done to him.

The immediate concern is how to help the victim believe that he can recover. In some communities, there may be professionals in rape-crisis centers, law enforcement, and counseling facilities who can provide immediate, short-term assistance to male victims. In other areas, however, there may be no one with the experience or resources to offer immediate assistance to males who are raped. In either case, many victims will need help for a much longer duration than can be provided by emergency services. That leaves you, one who is important to the victim, to remain constant and consistent over the long-term. This means that, over an extended period, you must balance your needs with his. You will find this charge to be both challenging and exhausting. As you learn to understand what it means to be sexually victimized, you will gain confidence in responding to his needs, while addressing your own.

Always remember that it took courage and trust for him to reveal to you that he has been raped. He revealed this because he trusts you. He wants to recover and needs your support. This book will help you to help him as he takes his first important steps toward recovery. You are to be commended for standing beside him.

# 2
# Facts and Myths

Understanding people's mistaken beliefs gives us insight into what is unique to males as opposed to females who are raped. For males in our culture, there are constant pressures to believe that to "be a man," one must never be out of control, always be strong, not be overly emotional, never be effeminate, and not be gay. To be raped by another male fundamentally challenges shared beliefs about what it means to be masculine. It causes the victim to have great self-doubt about being a man, it causes a corrosive self-blame about being victimized, and it often causes others to target him with harsh judgments. These harsh judgments of others often center around perceptions of the victim's sexual orientation. Unfortunately, misplaced concerns about the victim's sexuality only serve to make him feel confused and guilty about being victimized, while reducing his willingness to report the assault.

For a male rape victim who *is not gay*, the comments and actions of others may make him think that the reason for the rape is that he was perceived as gay or effeminate. This increases the likelihood that he will blame himself for being raped, rather than placing responsibility where it belongs, on the rapist. For a male rape victim who *is gay*, the tendency also is to place the blame on self because of one's sexual orientation rather than on the actions of the rapist. For a male victim who is questioning his sexual orientation, a rape at this time can be especially confusing and a source of self-blame. Regardless of a male victim's sexual orientation, he still is likely to blame himself for being weak, vulnerable, and not in control — characteristics that our culture says are not desirable for a "real man." In other words, if a boy or man is raped, he blames himself for not being "manly." It is, of course, a myth to believe that "real men" are never vulnerable, weak, or out of control.

There are other reasons why the male rape victim feels blame for being raped. One is the belief that we live in a fair and just world where people "reap what they sow," or "get what they deserve." This implies that if something bad happens, the person who was harmed caused it to happen. The implication for the victim is that others may think, "He must have had it coming." This makes it easier for others to scrutinize the behavior of a sexual-assault victim and to render harsh judgments of him. This happens even during rape trials where the victim is asked not only to testify about the facts of the case, but also to defend his innocence. The logic is simple. If we think that the victim was raped because he did something he should not have done, then he deserved the rape. This logic suggests that if we always behave appropriately, then we will never be vulnerable to rape.

Even if your friend or loved one feels that he made poor decisions in the circumstances leading to the rape, ask him this: Does making a poor decision constitute an offense deserving of rape? The answer, of course, is no it does not — not ever. He needs to know (and believe that you know) that there never is justification for someone to sexually assault another.

Because recovery from rape is impeded by myths that distort how people see the crime, the victim senses even unspoken criticism from others. He needs to know that you do not subscribe to the myths about rape that unfairly and incorrectly blame him. Rape is an extreme violation of a person. It destroys the very core of a person's well-being. With this in mind, it is important to help every male who is raped, regardless of his age or sexual orientation, to re-

8

gain his dignity and integrity by dispelling the basic myths about rape that cause him self-doubt.

## Myth One: "It Only Happens in Prison"

People frequently associate the rape of males with life in prison. While it is true that the sexual assault of males is a feature of prison culture, it is a mistake to assume that male rapes are limited to prisons. Although we lack reliable statistics that indicate every context in which males are raped by other males, we know that young and old alike can be the victim of rape in almost any setting. Rape can happen to young males in schools and in summer camps, it can happen to adult males at work or while at play, and it can happen to elderly males in nursing homes. Strangers, acquaintances, and caretakers alike can be perpetrators. Unfortunately, the mistaken belief that male rape happens only in prison has an important negative consequence for the victim. If he is courageous enough to divulge to authorities or to others that he was raped, he may not be believed. It violates conventional wisdom that a male, particularly an adult male, could be raped in a setting other than a prison. Even if he is believed, there may be doubts about his role in the victimization. Specifically, because the rape took place in a setting not usually associated with sexual violence, the victim's behavior may be viewed as a contributing factor.

## Myth Two: "He Asked for It"

Any implication that a male rape victim "asks for" or secretly enjoys rape is a myth. Victims *never* seek this terrible experience. This is true whether the victim is gay, bisexual, or heterosexual. Unfortunately, this myth is often reinforced if a victim exhibits no *visible* injuries. The absence of injuries suggests to others that the victim failed to resist and, therefore, must have consented. Rapists use violence or the threat of violence to overpower and to control their victims. Rapists sometimes use so-called "date rape" drugs

9

such as Rohypnol or GHB to incapacitate their victims and to impair their memories. Rapists may also use subtle forms of coercion to control their victims, even if overt force is not employed.

Consent is based upon the ability to freely choose, and the rapist does not offer his victim a choice. By its very definition, rape is a *nonconsensual* act. *Submitting* out of fear is never consent. Each rape victim does what he (or she) needed to do at the time in order to survive, even if the victim felt paralyzed by fear or recognized the futility of resistance.

Despite being forced to submit, many male victims of rape feel unnecessary guilt and self-doubt. For example, if the victim had an erection while being forcibly fondled sexually, he will likely struggle with the paradox of being aroused during an act that was done against his will. Because an erection is usually associated with sexual desire, this can create great confusion and guilt among victims. Bear in mind, adolescent and adult males may experience erections (and ejaculation) in very frightening circumstances, such as on the battlefield or in a fight. Remind him that anyone placed in a life-threatening situation may respond with involuntary physical reactions, but that these reactions do not, in any way, imply consent. An erection (and ejaculation) during a rape is neither an indication of consent, nor is it an indication that the victim enjoyed the experience.

If he senses that you think he contributed to the crime or that he enjoyed the experience, he will distance himself from you at a time when your support is needed the most. This could further hinder his recovery, and it could destroy your relationship.

## Myth Three: "Men Should Be Able to Prevent Their Rape"

We mistakenly believe that any male could have prevented the sexual assault by putting up a fight — the "manly thing to do." The implicit message here is that failure to fight off an attack is a sign of weakness or cowardice, which in our society is not "manly." Not only is the male victim's "manhood" in question following a same-sex attack, but his "manly" ability to defend himself is also doubted. Little wonder that so many male victims internalize this "deficiency" and feel a deep sense of guilt and shame. Perhaps this is why male victims frequently will endure the private hell of never divulging the truth of the rape, rather than suffer the humiliation and the stigma associated with judgments about their masculine identity and sexual orientation.

The belief that a male victim could have prevented the assault, however, ignores a basic reality: the threat of bodily harm or death overpowers the desire to defend oneself. The threat of being beaten or killed is real. Firearms, knives, clubs, and other weapons are used at a much higher rate when males are raped than when females are raped. This is because males who rape other males believe that their victims are likely to have more muscle power to resist, thus they often rely upon extreme threat and brutality to accomplish their ends. The rapist will often use weapons to control his male victim and to secure his own safety. As such, the risk of serious injury to a male victim is very real, especially if he attempts to fight off the attack.

Even if no physical weapon is used, males (like females) can be raped if the rapist uses extortion, subtle forms of coercion, deception, or psychological control. Such tactics by rapists where the threat is not based upon use of a weapon may be somewhat more common in two contexts: encounters in the gay community, and encounters involving young male victims and older perpetrators. An effective weapon to force someone into submission need not always be a gun or a knife. Certainly the law does not require that a weapon be used for an act to qualify as rape, nor does it require the victim to physically resist the attack. We should never judge any rape victim — male or female, gay or straight — for failure to physically resist the rapist.

11

# Myth Four: "It Was a Homosexual Act"

A common belief about same-sex rape is that it is a homosexual event (i.e., just another expression of "gay sex"). This belief is false. Same-sex rape is not a consensual sex act between gay men. Rape is *never* consensual, and it may or may not involve someone who is gay. In rape, sex is a vehicle through which anger, control, and violence are expressed. It is not a form of desired sexual intimacy. Even if the victim is gay, same-sex rape is a traumatic experience that does not in any way represent a desired sexual encounter.

Another negative aspect of this myth is more complex because it is rooted in fear, resentment, and hatred of homosexuality, and, by implication, of persons who are gay. Such fear and hatred of gay people is called "homophobia," and it has several unfortunate consequences. Ironically, one consequence of homophobia is that it can be a motive for rape. A person or group motivated by the hatred of homosexuals may sexually assault a person who is thought to be gay.

Most often males who rape other males think of themselves as *heterosexual* in their basic sexual orientation. While it is true that the equivalent of "date rape" occurs in the gay community, the more typical same-sex rape of a male involves a perpetrator who defines himself as heterosexual in orientation. How could fear, resentment, and hatred of homosexuality motivate heterosexual males to be sexually violent toward other males? The answer, in part, has to do with how some males behave when they are immersed in predominately male environments in which powerful peers are homophobic. In male environments, such as prisons, military camps, fraternities, boarding schools, and athletic teams, demonstrating physical power over another is a way for some males to validate their masculinity. Because rape is an act of domination through which the victim is controlled and humiliated, some perpetrators use it to enhance their status among certain other males, es-

12

pecially if the victim is perceived to be gay or otherwise less than "manly" in the eyes of the male group.

Often such rapes, including gang rapes, occur in the context of hazing or other initiation rites associated with all-male groups. Under such circumstances, taunting and sadistic forms of sexual violation, such as forcing objects into the victim's anus are common. Thus, for some males, rape in this context can serve one or more of three purposes: 1) demonstrating one's power and superiority through domination and humiliation of another; 2) achieving group acceptance by weathering an initiation rite; and 3) publicly demonstrating one's heterosexuality by expressing hatred directed toward males thought to be gay, effeminate, or otherwise less than "manly." For these violent and homophobic male predators, sexual violence toward gay men creates social distance between them and their victims. In their minds, the assault "proves" that the rapist could not be "one of them" because he is openly demonstrating to himself and to others that he hates gays. Homophobia helps to set the stage for the rape of males by other males. When rape is based on hatred of gay men, it quite literally constitutes a hate crime.

Another consequence of resentment toward homosexuals is that it tends to cause male victims of rape to be viewed as gay, whether or not they are homosexual. There is great stigma attached to the label of "homosexual," and this stigma can negatively affect how others treat male victims, thus impeding their recovery. Because of this stigma, heterosexual victims are unlikely to seek help because they do not want their sexual identity to be questioned by others. Gay male victims are likewise silenced for fear that their sexual identity will be made public, thus causing them to suffer the prejudices of others. In either case, homophobia has the negative effect of silencing male victims of same-sex rape, thus reducing the likelihood that they will receive help or that the perpetrator will be caught.

Regardless of whether a male is gay, bisexual, or heterosexual, his sexuality and "manhood" are called into question if he is raped.

The terror of rape is compounded by the stigma of being emasculated and devalued in the eyes of others. Questions about the victim's sexual identity and about his possible complicity in the act often color how others see him. Sadly, such questions also affect how he may see himself. Most male victims, regardless of their sexual orientation, begin to have doubts about their sexuality in the aftermath of the rape. Even male children who are raped by older males have fears and questions about their emerging sexuality. Given that others doubt the victim's sexual identity, too often the tendency is to distance themselves from the victim at a time when their support and reassurance is most needed. In addition, if the victim believes that the rapist was homosexual, then his own homophobia may be generalized to the point where he blames gay men for the rape and fantasizes about "getting even" with all gay people.

## Myth Five: "It Is Humorous When a Male Is Raped"

Sadly, a common reaction of others, particularly other males, is to make "funny" remarks when they learn that a male was raped. This tendency to see humor in male rape is less when young children are victims and more common when adolescents and adults are raped. Perhaps this is because children evoke sympathy and are seen as blameless when they are harmed. For older victims, however, the response toward them is different. Time and again there seems to be an irresistible urge for male peers to crack sexually-explicit and homophobic "jokes" about the same-sex assault of another man.

Why does male rape elicit such a response? It is probably true that humor in this situation is a way for male friends to relieve their discomfort at the thought of a fellow male being raped. Humor also may be a way of showing others that one is not gay. It also is probably true that "humorous remarks" about male rape are not meant to harm the victim.

Regardless of intent, however, it is important to understand how such remarks are seen by the victim. When others find humor in male rape, the victim feels as if he is alone and that no one understands what he is going through. It makes him reluctant to trust anyone with his thoughts and feelings about what has happened. It makes him wonder about who his true friends are. And finally, it reinforces his worst doubts about who he is and what the rape means in his life. Thus, it is important that you do not treat his rape as a source of humor, and it is important that you discourage others from doing so. Remind these persons of a basic truth: criminal violence is not funny, and rape is both criminal and violent.

## Overcoming the Myths

In order to facilitate the victim's recovery, reinforce several basic messages. Tell him you do not believe that same-sex rape constitutes a homosexual encounter. Acknowledge that fear of homosexuality has the unfortunate consequence of silencing victims and of causing others to respond inappropriately. Reassure him that you do not doubt his masculinity. Help him to understand that rape is an act of violence, and that it has nothing to do with his sexuality, even though sexual activity occurred. And tell him that you will consistently convey these messages to others who know of the event and who raise questions about it.

It also is important for you to encourage him to question his self-doubts and to focus on what is true. He did not ask to be raped. He did not enjoy it. He did not consent. His sexuality is not the issue and neither is his "manhood." The issue is clear: *he is the victim of a crime.* Your consistent reassurance that you do not accept homophobic biases and cultural myths about rape, and that you will discourage such biases in others, will help to quell his doubts.

# 3
# Addressing
# Immediate Concerns

While no two rape victims are alike, there are two common elements in all rapes. First, rape is a traumatic experience that requires time for victims to recover. Second, those personally close to the victim are profoundly affected by the assault. You can help by:

- believing him and listening to him
- knowing what to expect and helping him to understand what is happening
- accepting his feelings and recognizing his strengths
- communicating compassion and acceptance
- encouraging him to make decisions that help him to regain control
- treating his fears and concerns as understandable responses
- working to diminish his feelings of being isolated and alone
- holding realistic expectations, especially when he becomes frustrated or impatient
- helping him to identify resources and support persons
- being yourself and standing by him

These messages provide what the male rape victim needs — unconditional support by family and friends. If you consistently send these messages, you will help to set the stage for his recovery.

The period immediately after the sexual assault is an emotionally charged, confusing, and anxious time. The victim has been terrorized and totally violated, and now he faces additional worries. For example, he is now likely to ask himself questions such as:

- Am I safe now?
- Do I need medical attention?
- Do I report this to the police?
- Did I contract a sexually-transmitted infection such as syphilis or HIV?
- Should I tell anyone?
- What will my family and friends think?
- What will I do when others find out?
- How does this affect my sexuality?
- How will this affect those I love?
- Will my life ever be normal?
- Am I still a "man"?

In addition to these questions, there are many other concerns. These could include:

- Does he have personal leave or sick days he can use to take time off from work?
- Can he afford counseling?
- When, and under what circumstances, should family and others be told about what happened?
- Will he want to file a civil suit or perhaps initiate a criminal case? Does he need an attorney?

- Will he want to relocate for safety reasons, and what are his options?
- If things were stolen during the attack, does he have the money to replace them?
- If the case has been publicized, does he know his rights with the media?

The emotional consequences of sexual assault continue well beyond the attack. Unfortunately, medical and legal professionals may unintentionally contribute to the victim's trauma as they routinely conduct their investigation. For example, if he decides to immediately report being raped, he will be asked (for legal reasons) to undergo an invasive physical exam before he changes clothes, bathes, eats, drinks, smokes, combs his hair, or chews gum, and if possible, before he urinates or defecates.* Moreover, he may have to recount the incident several times in detail to the police and to prosecutors, all of whom are strangers.

The rape exam itself is often a frightening experience. The process begins by obtaining an account of the incident followed by an external examination of the rape victim. Signs of lacerations, bruising, abrasions, redness, and swelling, as well as bite marks and secretions are documented. Most males have never undergone an exam such as an endoscopy where a medical instrument is inserted up the rectum. This can be both painful and terrifying if the victim suffered anal penetration by the rapist. A swab of the urethral orifice for the purpose of determining the presence of a sexually transmitted infection also is routine protocol. Photographs of the genital area may be taken. Combing of pubic and facial hair also is customary. Testing for the presence of alcohol and drugs

---

*Because physical evidence does not stay viable for long, rape exams ideally should be conducted within 24 to 48 hours of the attack. If a person who is raped is unsure about reporting the crime to law enforcement, you might inform him of the limited time he has before the relevant evidence is permanently lost. It is usually better to have such evidence collected early, in case he later chooses to help prosecute.

such as Rohypnol (often known as a "date rape" drug) is common. Even though these are necessary procedures for gathering evidence and for evaluating injury, they may seem invasive and like another violation from the victim's perspective. To minimize the victim's trauma, it is critically important that each step in the medical exam be explained beforehand and conducted with sensitivity.

While it is true that rules of evidence require detailed questioning by police, this examination may appear to the victim as both unnecessary and as another personal attack. He may be especially reluctant to discuss certain elements of the rape, such as suffering anal penetration or being forced to place the perpetrator's penis in his mouth. At the very moment he needs sympathetic understanding, these impersonal but necessary procedures can add to his fears and his humiliation. The following illustrate the kinds of problems he may confront:

- *Callous responses* from law enforcement or medical personnel.
- *Scrutiny of his sexual orientation* by those taking the report and by others.
- *Stigma* associated with the myth that "males are not victims" or should be able to "put up a fight."
- *Value conflicts* if his lifestyle and conduct clash with the religious beliefs of others.
- *Loss of independence*, especially if he is an adolescent.

These are understandable reasons why male victims of rape do not report the crime to authorities or to their family members and friends. And when they do report it, they may not want to *fully* disclose the sexually explicit details of the rape for fear of being blamed, humiliated, or judged. Yet, even if the victim is reluctant to talk about the experience, he still needs to be examined by a physician. Because many sexually-transmitted diseases have an incubation period, encourage him to return to his physician two to three weeks after the assault for follow-up tests and to further evaluate any physical injuries. (Testing for HIV should be anonymous and is neither necessary nor appropriate during the initial medical exam.) Helping the victim to receive medical attention conveys the message that you believe his account of what happened and that you take the assault seriously. You are, therefore, communicating powerful support by letting him know that he will not face this time alone. In addition, if he later changes his mind and decides to report the rape to authorities, the medical evidence will be invaluable.

# 4
# What You Should Do

The time immediately after the sexual assault, where either damaging forces or positive influences are set in motion, requires great care on your part. The things most needed at this time are *gentleness* and *acceptance*. To positively affect his recovery, there are a number of things you should and should not do.

## Do

- Refrain from unintentionally humiliating him by prying into the physically-intimate aspects of the rape. Allow him to discuss such issues when he is ready.

- Reassure him that he is not responsible for being raped. It is important for him to know that you do not equate the attack with bad judgment or weakness.

- Encourage him to discuss, when he is ready, any beliefs and self-doubts he has about being raped. Help him to put the blame where it belongs . . . on the perpetrator.

- Allow him to regain some control by encouraging him to make small decisions and then larger ones. This process can begin by asking him ordinary questions that simply provide him a choice, such as, "Would you like a hot meal?" "Would you want me to call in sick for you?" "Would you prefer that I drive?" These simple questions encourage decision making, which helps the victim regain a sense of control over his life.

- Assure him that he is not alone. He needs to know, regardless of what happened, that your relationship will remain intact.

## Do Not

- Do not tell him that you will "get" the rapist because this will cause him to fear for *your* safety.

- Do not encourage or support any thoughts of his "getting even" with the rapist by acting outside of the law. (Male victims of rape are especially prone to consider retaliation. Seeking revenge, however, places him at risk of serious legal problems or additional injury.)

- Do not let your anger about what happened shift attention away from his needs to your concerns.

- Do not make him feel that talking about the incident will upset you or that he is "imposing" an emotional burden on you.

- Do not tell him that his concerns about his sexuality brought on by the rape make you uncomfortable. Expressing such discomfort may confuse him further and cause him to feel that no one can be trusted with the thoughts that may be troubling him the most.

- Do not direct your anger toward him, even if he seems unresponsive to you.

- Do not ask questions that even hint that he is to blame. A safe rule is to avoid questions that begin with the word "why." Examples of questions to avoid are: "Why did you go there?" "Why didn't you yell?" "Why didn't you fight him?" "Why did you talk to him in the first place?"

- Do not make decisions for him or demand that he follow a particular course of action. (The one exception is that you should strongly encourage him to seek medical attention.)
- Do not imply, at any time, that he may have enjoyed the experience.
- Do not tell the victim that everything is all right when everything is *not* all right. Avoid minimizing the gravity of what has happened, because such a response suggests that you cannot deal with the situation.
- Do not touch or hold him without asking permission or unless he shows signs that such comfort is welcome.
- Do not try to lift his spirits by making jokes about what has happened.
- Do not tell him you know how he feels. Only he truly knows.

Keep in mind that no one response is typical of all males who experience a sexual assault. Initially, most (not all) rape victims experience deep shame and self-doubt that may reduce their willingness to speak openly. Additionally, most feel that they should be able to "handle it themselves" without "burdening" others with their troubles. By being patient, approachable, tolerant, and nonjudgmental, you will create a climate in which he will eventually feel safe enough to share his pain.

# Long-Term Communication Strategies

Discussing the assault can be a major source of anxiety for males who are raped, yet effective communication is important to his long-term adjustment and to the survival of valued relationships. Unfortunately, many relationships undergo severe strain in the aftermath of an assault. Communication is disrupted, people feel frustrated and helpless, and there may be mutual feelings of resentment. Despite the emotional turmoil you both are experiencing, there are several steps you can take to promote effective communication.

- Respect his fear. Offenders commonly threaten to seriously harm their victims if the victims do not comply or if they tell anyone what happened. Although this fear remains long after the sexual assault, male victims especially are reluctant to admit that they are afraid. Tell him that fear is a normal and understandable reaction, and that being fearful does not make him a coward. Indeed, admitting fear is an indication of trust and is a positive step toward overcoming that fear.

- Accept his strong feelings and his mood swings, and remain consistent in your support.

- Be patient. Listen without being critical and without giving unsolicited advice. Give him the opportunity to express his feelings at a pace that is comfortable to him. If he is reluctant to talk, do not become angry.

- Do not pressure him to self-disclose or "interrogate" him by insisting that he recount the details of the incident repeatedly. Forcing him to be candid may cause resentment and withdrawal.

- Do not express anger or accuse him of "hiding something" because he did not tell you sooner, or because he failed to divulge all the details up front. Silence provides a normal way for him to sort through the traumatic experience. Silence is not rejection of you.

- Pay special attention to recurring themes in conversations. These might be clues that provide insight into issues that are troubling him. Sexual assault can bring out much "unfinished business," including problems that existed before the assault.

- If the victim is gay, do not use his victimization as an opportunity to try and get him to "change" his sexual orientation. Family members who are upset about the victim's sexual orientation and his associations are especially prone to do this. It will only hurt his recovery and your relationship with him by making comments such as, "See what can happen by hanging out in those places and with those people!" The rape of a male should never be treated as an opportunity to create a forum on the victim's sexuality.

- Eventually, the two of you should discuss the impact of the attack on your relationship. It is important that you talk about how the relationship is being affected because the emotional consequences of sexual assault are traumatic for everyone. Calmly sharing your feelings and your vulnerabilities will promote the mutual nurturing that aids the recovery process.

Perhaps the most difficult challenge is to avoid being drawn into conflicts that are rooted in his emotional turmoil. Whether it is silence, mood swings, or a persistent anger on his part, it is important that you remain consistent in your support. There are times, however, when it is perfectly acceptable for you to make a space for yourself, especially if the alternative is to get caught up in an argument with him. Have faith that, with your love and support, his emotional turmoil will subside.

# 5
# What to Say to Others

When someone is sexually assaulted, close friends and family members frequently respond in ways that mirror those of the victim: shock, denial, anger, confusion, guilt, and helplessness. These reactions reflect attempts to make sense out of a senseless event. Therefore, it is important for all of you to talk about and work through your feelings.

In talking through what has happened, however, there is a tendency for some people to make well-intentioned comments that are based upon their misconceptions about rape. Such comments can have the effect of increasing, rather than reducing, the rape victim's emotional burden. You can help by serving as a "buffer" between the victim and others. There are a number of ways in which to do this without alienating others, including the following:

- Discourage family and friends from threatening revenge against the attacker. Such threats arise partly out of a sincere desire to affirm their support for the victim and partly to counteract their own feelings of helplessness. Threats, however, do little to reassure rape victims and do much to cause further trauma. For example, the victim may worry about the safety of family members who declare their intentions to "pay back" the attacker. These threats could also complicate any dealings he may have with law enforcement authorities.

- Be careful of how you and others attempt to reduce tension. Friends and family members may joke about a male being raped by another male in an effort to ease the tension. Male friends especially may be inclined to handle their discomfort with the rape through "funny" remarks, including comments that express a homophobic theme. Advise them that such attempts at "humor" are inappropriate and hurtful. Inappropriate humor is likely to increase the victim's confusion and isolation and, perhaps, to cause him to distrust those who truly want to be helpful. Inappropriate humor also may serve to reinforce his deepest fears about how his sexuality is being perceived by others.

- Respect the victim's wishes for confidentiality. He alone should decide with whom and under what circumstances to discuss his feelings. Remember, in the aftermath of rape, victims tend to be reluctant to discuss their feelings about the attack. This reluctance reflects their initial attempts to come to grips with what has happened and to deal with their confusion. It also is rooted in feelings of shame or embarrassment. Others, however, may interpret such reluctance to talk as unhealthy withdrawal or as a sign that the rape incident is "eating away at him." In a well-intended effort to be helpful, others might then solicit *without the victim's permission* assistance from co-workers, clergy, or mental health professionals. Such attempts to intervene, unless requested by the victim, can aggravate his emotional distress, and they should be discouraged.

- Empower the victim; do not try to control or to overprotect him. Dissuade others from trying to "protect" the victim by suggesting that he move back home or to another city, curtail social activities, or otherwise be "extra careful" at all times. Apart from the security needs of young children, there should not be the equivalent of 24-hour

30

surveillance of the rape victim. Such monitoring could un-intentionally reinforce his feelings of vulnerability and powerlessness. In short, this kind of "support" could hinder the victim's efforts to recover and may undermine his ability to cope effectively.

- Let the victim decide when a "distraction" is appropriate and necessary. Despite what some may believe, the rape victim will not recover from an attack simply because others do things to "take his mind off of it" (e.g., by running errands with him, taking him on shopping trips, or going to movies with him). Such distractions could be an imposition. Similarly, engaging in a "friendly conspiracy" with others to keep the victim's mind off the rape by acting as if it never happened, is counterproductive. The victim could mistake these diversions to mean that his family and friends regard the assault as too awful to discuss or too trivial to acknowledge. True, there are times when a victim wants to engage in these distracting activities, but it should be at the victim's request. Take your cues from him and encourage others to do so as well.

- Remind family and friends that the rape victim has privacy needs, and that when he expresses the desire to be alone, this desire should be respected. Sometimes a constant stream of well-wishers will be an emotional drain. In respecting the victim's wish for privacy, you will send two empowering messages: he is the best judge of what he needs, and he has the strength to help himself get better.

- Remind others that they should not imply, in any way, that the attack was caused by what the victim did or did not do. It is crucial that you help others to understand that it is impossible for them to know what the victim should or should not have done to prevent the rape. This is particularly true in cases involving younger males who are assaulted by a person whom they know and trust. Such

second-guessing is a form of "victim blaming" that reinforces guilt and self-blame.

- Encourage discussions about the nature and negative consequences of homophobia. Viewing same-sex rape
through the distorted lens of homophobia only harms victims.

As someone who cares about the victim's recovery, use your
contacts with others to establish an accepting, nonjudgmental climate in which he can express his painful feelings to others without
fear of criticism. The victim needs to know that his family and
friends do not hold him responsible for what happened, and that
because he survived the assault, his decisions were the right ones.

# 6
# Long-Term Consequences

The effects of sexual assault linger far beyond the attack and its immediate aftermath. For some, a complete resolution may take months or even years. Rape is an all-consuming event for victims, at least for a period of time. It can dominate one's thoughts and cast a dark shroud over one's emotional state. If you think of rape as a profoundly violent invasion, both physical and psychological, then you can begin to understand the highly personal nature of this crime and the reasons for its residual effects. No one is ever fully prepared for the upheaval rape causes.

From research, we know that the rape recovery process unfolds over time.* Although much of our understanding of the traumatic consequences of sexual violence is derived from research on female victims of rape, there is every reason to believe that the experience also is traumatic for male victims.

---

*In the 1970s, researchers and therapists identified a series of symptoms and reactions that many rape victims experience on the road to recovery. These reactions are referred to as *Rape Trauma Syndrome*. More recently, researchers and mental health professionals have expanded this framework for examining rape recovery. Increasingly, they are describing and treating rape victims within the framework of the diagnostic category called *Post-traumatic Stress Disorder*.

While no two survivors of rape necessarily go through the same sequence of experiences as they struggle to recover, there are common elements in the recovery process. One issue of concern has its origins in an event that occurs immediately *before* the rape. Victims of sexual assault commonly experience *preimpact terror.* These are the very frightening moments just prior to the assault, when the victim knows what is about to happen but is powerless to stop it.

The courts recognize preimpact terror as a legitimate concern. In civil court, for example, special damages can be awarded to the families of airplane-crash victims for the period of time the passengers know the plane is going to crash . . . until it does. These damages are based upon emotional injuries associated with the extreme terror experienced when the passenger realizes that a crash is imminent. Males who are raped by other males also experience this kind of terror, but the impending devastation is *deliberate,* not accidental. For example, a first-time resident of a juvenile detention facility will likely experience such terror. Others in the facility tell him graphically and with embellishment that he will be raped at the earliest opportunity. During this preattack phase, the juvenile can neither fully believe nor fully deny what is about to happen. His mind floods with thoughts. In essence, he is bombarded by waves of *conflicting* ideas: denial on the one hand, defeat on the other. Just as the assault is about to happen, he realizes with certainty there is no escape and that he may never be the same again.

Understanding the existence of preimpact terror is important to the recovery process. The victim's feelings of guilt, shame, and self-doubt in the aftermath of rape shatter his male identity. The victim is likely to relive the moments before the attack and second guess himself because he was unable to stop what was happening. Men are, after all, expected to defend themselves, and "only cowards and weaklings fail to do so," the victim tells himself. No matter that he was frightened for his life, the victim wrestles with what he could have done to prevent this ultimate dishonor. In other

34

words, in reliving the event, he imposes upon himself an unreasonable standard of conduct based upon guilt-ridden speculation about how he could or should have responded to the threat. However logical or reasonable such a standard of conduct may seem to him in retrospect (when he is safe), the reality is that, as the assault progressed, *he was powerless and in a state of terror.* Is it reasonable for him to think logically under such circumstances? Of course not. Yet, he reflects upon the moments just before the attack, *while he was in a state of preimpact terror,* and judges himself as a failure. He applies to himself a heavy-handed standard of "maleness" that denies the life-threatening risk he faced during the attack.

After the rape, the victim typically experiences a number of other symptoms. *Acute distress* is common immediately after the attack. The symptoms may include shock, disbelief, confusion, anxiety, crying, humiliation, irritation, and other signs of emotional disorganization. The victim may *appear* to be extremely controlled on the surface, but he is masking more troubling emotions at a deeper level. At the same time, the victim may exhibit soreness and bruising from the attack, rectal bleeding, tension headaches, fatigue, sleep disturbances, nausea, and lack of appetite.

The victim also may experience a variety of other feelings in the weeks after the rape: fear, anger, revenge fantasies, embarrassment, and depression, as well as a festering sense of shame and self-blame. Abrupt changes in mood are common. Some victims may feel they are overreacting to normal everyday problems, which increases their distress. They are on an emotional roller coaster. They seem on the verge of extremes, sometimes near rage, sometimes near tears.

During this phase, it is important for you to remember that these physical and emotional reactions are *normal* responses to a terrifying, life-threatening experience and to the inappropriate responses of others. When the victim exhibits these fears and symptoms, let him know these feelings are understandable, and that such feelings do not mean he is "going crazy."

Gradually the victim will enter a period of *apparent* readjustment. During this stage, he may announce that the incident has been forgotten and give every indication that it is no longer troubling. His resoluteness may appear to be a sign of full recovery, but, typically, it is not. If anything, the assault lingers in the background of his thoughts while he attempts to make sense of what has happened. It is during this apparent readjustment that the victim may contemplate suicide or drink heavily, particularly if he lacks solid support from family and friends. Without an effective support system, the risk of succumbing to alcohol or to a suicidal impulse is greatly increased.

During this "outward adjustment" period, the victim may fluctuate between denial of his depression and acute fear of the circumstances that trigger memories of the assault. It is important to remember that such denial is not a sign of stubbornness or weakness, nor is it, in the short run, self-destructive. Instead, denial allows him to control the pace of his recovery so he will not be overwhelmed by an onslaught of images and emotions.

Eventually, the victim may experience a seemingly abrupt reemergence of assault-related memories. Disturbing though the memories may be, their emergence represents a transition to the final phase of recovery, or *integration*. The initial sign of integration is a return of the troubling responses that he may have experienced earlier (e.g., depression, anxiety, eating disturbances, insomnia, nightmares, tension, headaches). A victim's emotional turmoil may surface in ways that are disquieting and perhaps unpredictable. Remember, if the victim feels unsupported, he may externalize his trauma through aggression or internalize his distress to the point of suicidal thoughts, reverting to the previous stage of apparent readjustment. Many relationships undergo the greatest period of stress at this point because the victim appears to be getting worse, not better. These responses, while understandably upsetting to you and to other family members and friends, may be a not-so-silent announcement that your friend or loved one is beginning to process

36

and to integrate images and feelings associated with the attack. Simply stated, he is coming to terms with what has happened so that he may get on with his life.

In addition to the distress that such images and feelings may have on those around him, *he* may feel as if his progress is going in reverse, instead of going forward. These feelings, however, are largely an "echo" of his initial responses, in that they are not experienced with the same intensity or duration as before. Because they are less intense than before, these feelings are somewhat easier for him to manage.

## The Significance of Flashbacks

Throughout the recovery process, there is a particular kind of troubling thought pattern that many male victims experience, but few care to voice. Male victims of same-sex rape tend to have sexually-graphic flashbacks of the rape. Sometimes these flashbacks develop into vivid sexual imagery involving males generally. These flashbacks are *not* similar to the sexual fantasies that most people experience. One important difference between fantasies and vivid flashbacks is that the person can control a sexual fantasy. A flashback, however, seems to control the victim. The sexual imagery of a flashback seems to come out of nowhere and strike like a thunderbolt. Certain sights, smells, sounds, or other sensory stimulation that corresponds to the rape event can trigger the flashback. The mental image that is triggered *intrudes* itself upon the victim *despite the victim's wishes to make it stop*. The flashback may be so powerful that it is almost as if the victim is reliving the traumatic event. For victims who experience a flashback, it takes great determination to shake off such powerful imagery and to regain control.

Another difference is that sexual fantasies are a source of pleasure. The graphic sexual flashbacks from the rape are not pleasurable. They are frightening and confusing, rather like a panic attack.

Such images are not something that the victim wants to think about. It is the persistent and intrusive nature of these troubling flashbacks that often complicates aspects of the victim's recovery.

How do flashbacks affect male victims of rape? To answer this, one must understand the subtle link between sexual flashbacks and deep-seated fears male victims have about their sexuality in the aftermath of the rape. The fact that some male victims have these flashbacks, or that flashbacks can develop into intrusive sexual imagery involving males in general, causes victims to doubt their sexual orientation and their sexual adequacy. Because such images seep into a victim's consciousness, he begins to wonder if these thoughts mean he is having sexual *feelings* for males in general, or for his rapist in particular. In other words, *unwanted and intrusive sexual thoughts are confused for sexual attractions and desires typical of a fantasy.* Even though the origin of such thoughts is not based upon a fantasy that the victim is choosing, and even though these are not pleasurable thoughts, the victim believes that having such thoughts must mean that he is *attracted* to them. A heterosexual victim, for example, might interpret such thoughts to mean that he is becoming gay. After all, he reasons, he never had such thoughts before the experience of being raped by someone of the same sex. Simply stated, he confuses *intrusive thoughts about* with *fantasy feelings for* the object of his imagination. For a heterosexual male, this confusion grows into a profound fear that he must be turning gay.

For a gay male victim of rape, there is similar confusion about the meaning of this intrusive sexual imagery. Having vivid sexual flashbacks of the rape may be interpreted by the victim to mean that he must have somehow desired or wanted to be raped, and that he is therefore responsible. Because of these thoughts, he also may fear that sadistic sexual violence is something he will seek in future encounters.

Regardless of the victim's sexual orientation, these intrusive thoughts cause confusion and fear. Almost without exception, male victims want such thoughts to go away and are afraid that their sexuality has changed fundamentally by virtue of the fact that they are having these unwanted thoughts. To help the male victim cope with flashbacks, both you and he need to understand the following:

- Graphic sexual thoughts following the rape are relatively common.

- Intrusive sexual imagery involving a person of the same sex does not mean that the victim's sexual identity is changed, or changing.

- Having flashbacks does not mean that one is attracted to the rapist or "subconsciously desires" to be the target of sexual violence.

- Having sexually-graphic flashbacks does not mean that one is going crazy.

- These intrusive thoughts go to the heart of the victim's deepest fears, and it is understandable why he may not want to reveal that he is having such thoughts.

- Over time, as the victim gains more control and learns what triggers graphic memories of the rape, the flashbacks will subside.

## Encouraging His Recovery

Recovery from rape is something like taking "three steps forward, two steps back." Recovery is not necessarily a discrete series of stages that all victims go through in a sequential manner. Rape victims often fluctuate dramatically and unpredictably between recovery phases. This can be frustrating and confusing to all. To encourage his full recovery, there are several things that supporters should and should not do. These will further build upon our earlier suggestions about what should and should not be done in the immediate aftermath of the assault.

- Do not tell him that he "shouldn't think about the incident," or "shouldn't feel that way," or that he "should be over it by now." He cannot will himself to ignore troublesome images or to bury powerful feelings. Suggesting that he attempt to do so will undermine communication and will hinder his recovery. In general, avoid using the word "should" in your discussions with him.

- Acknowledge that graphic sexual flashbacks and panic attacks do not mean he should fear that some fundamental change in his sexuality is occurring. Reassure him that such flashbacks are a common yet temporary consequence of the rape. Encourage him to talk about those things that may trigger a flashback, because identifying and talking about these triggers can reduce one's vulnerability to them. Let him know also that if he wishes, you will listen in a nonjudgmental way to any flashback imagery he feels able to discuss.

- Do not become irritated because he has needs that place additional demands on you. He is reaching out to you, not because he wants to burden you unnecessarily, but because you are a person upon whom he can rely for understanding and support.

- Do not be upset if he *refuses* to accept help that you or others may offer. For many male victims of rape, accepting help seems to be an admission of weakness. Constant offers of help, though well-intended, can seem like a burden. Many males will absolutely refuse to go through counseling, even though this may be beneficial to them. Do not demand that the victim "get help" or constantly badger him about the counseling option. A better strategy is to provide him with helpful materials that he can read or view on his own. Most rape-crisis or counseling centers have such materials available. If he finds this material to be of value, then he may willingly accept additional help.

40

- Do not be angry if his recovery seems too slow. Remember, rape victims recover at different rates and in different ways. Try not to impose your terms of recovery on him. Such an imposition communicates a lack of understanding, rather than compassion, and it is likely to cause resentment.

- Consider doing the kind of joint activities that brought you closer together in the past. For most rape victims, a sharp dividing line now exists between their pre- and post-assault memories. Engaging in joint activities gives *both* of you opportunities to rediscover those positive, shared memories that constitute the *preassault* foundations of your relationship, and helps ensure that your relationship will endure the difficult days ahead.

- When it is appropriate and mutually agreed upon, seek the companionship of friends who are healthy and up-beat. The good cheer you experience from being around positive people provides a needed respite for both of you.

- Do not act in violent ways in the mistaken belief that violence is a good release for pent-up anger. Similarly, turning to alcohol does not eliminate feelings of anger. If anything, violence and alcohol consumption harm the relationship and are destructive. Furthermore, because the victim may recoil from anything or anyone associated with violence, violent behavior on your part will serve only to isolate him from you.

- Find a trusted person with whom *you* can talk without fear of being judged. For some, it is especially useful to locate support groups in which members meet regularly to discuss their experiences and strategies for healing. Such groups are often available through rape-crisis centers. Knowing that others have endured what you are going through can provide hope.

These suggestions should help you to realize two things. First, each person has a unique way of coping with stress, and each person needs the opportunity to recover on his own terms. Second, with patience, mutual support and openness, you will *both* recover and may succeed in building a relationship that is even *stronger,* because you endured a crisis *together*.

# 7
# Guidelines for Partners

One major consequence of your partner's rape are the feelings of anxiety about sexual activity. His being raped may result in a long-term fear of sexual involvement, a diminished sexual desire, a feeling that he has been rendered "asexual," or the rape may aggravate sexual difficulties that already existed between you. Such difficulties may be especially acute if the attack was extremely violent or involved multiple assailants. Moreover, problems in resuming sexual activity can be experienced by any male victim, *regardless of his sexual orientation.*

Caution is in order if the two of you are to resume a satisfying sexual relationship. Being insensitive to your partner's needs may make the resumption of sex seem rape-like or uncaring. The male victim may equate intimacy with being vulnerable, and he may wish to avoid being vulnerable. In addition, it is not uncommon for a rape victim to have flashbacks of the rape during *consensual* sexual relations, though he may be reluctant to reveal these flashbacks to you. The following suggestions will help.

- Give your partner every opportunity to regain a sense of personal control, especially in the area of sexual decision making. Do not demand or pressure him into sexual activity. A return to sexual activity may *seem* like a behavioral indicator that things are back to normal, even though they are not. It is almost as if one or both of you are saying,

"See, we are having sex again, so things must be okay." Unless he is ready for the resumption of sex, the act of love-making may serve to diminish his sexual desire and to complicate your relationship.

- Do not be angry with your partner if he appears less sexually responsive than he was before the rape. It may be that certain cues during intimacy remind him of the sexual assault (e.g., the smell of alcohol or the presence of drugs). The willingness to talk honestly about such troubling associations and the willingness to alter patterns that remind him of the attack will help your relationship.

- Just as you should not pressure your partner into an early resumption of sex, neither should you avoid any display of intimacy. Understandably, you may assume your partner has a diminished interest in sex, and you may, therefore, be tempted to step back out of consideration for him. But it is important that the victim not interpret your behavior as a sign that you feel he is "tarnished" by the rape or less appealing than before. Many victims of rape fear that their partners will see them as "damaged goods." There are many ways to express intimacy (e.g., hugging; non-sexual touching) without consummating sexual activity. Again, honest communication and your willingness to take cues from him and to alter your behavior will help.

- Be patient. Sexual disruption following an assault usually is temporary. If problems persist, counseling may be helpful.

One other issue is worth noting. In the aftermath of rape, some male victims become insensitive to the needs and feelings of their partners. Some may even become violent toward their partners. For some heterosexual males who are rape victims, there may be a tendency to "prove their manhood" by engaging in callous sexual conduct with females. Such conduct may include frequent sexual encounters with other women.

Because we do not believe that being a victim of a sex crime is justification for exploiting others, relationship counseling may be needed for his successful recovery. It is important that you be honest about your willingness to be supportive of him, but at the least, it also is important that you clarify boundaries so you do not place yourself in a position of potential harm.

# 8
# Guidelines for Parents

Sexual abuse of a child or adolescent involves perpetrators using any combination of deception, trickery, physical force, bribery,
and abuse of authority. Almost without exception, the perpetrator
will manipulate the situation so that the child or adolescent feels as
if he is to blame for the abuse. The feeling that he is to blame
makes it very difficult for the victim to report what has happened,
or to talk about the victimization once it is discovered.

In molesting young males, perpetrators often follow a pattern.
Typically there is a gradual build-up of personal contact in which
the victim is prepared over time. This contact often involves be-
friending the target, followed by subtle physical contact where the
victim is inappropriately touched "accidentally" in order to evaluate his vulnerability and to desensitize him. Perpetrators are highly
skilled at judging their victims' vulnerabilities. If the child or adolescent withdraws or seems afraid of the physical encroachment,
the sexual predator will downplay the touching and deliberately attempt to confuse the victim. Comments by the perpetrator such as
"Come on, it's okay, we are friends" or "Everyone does this," or
"This is just a fun game," are common. Rewards of money or gifts
for compliance and secrecy also are part of how the victim is ma-
nipulated. The perpetrator may also play upon the victim's insecu-
rities by laughing at him or challenging him to be brave and risk
doing something secret. The goal is to entice the victim to disre-

gard his feelings of caution by trusting the perpetrator and also to make the victim believe that he is responsible. Compliance also may be secured by a direct threat, but usually the manipulation is more subtle, through the use of words and bribes.

Whatever methods were used to manipulate your son, remember this: he was violated physically and psychologically, he was lied to by a person whom he may have trusted, he was made to feel responsible for the sexual violation, and he probably blames himself for what has happened. In general, the longer the abuse continued and the closer the perpetrator was to the victim, the more severe the emotional turmoil. Depending upon the victim's level of social and emotional development, he may feel guilty for trusting the abuser and for "allowing" himself to be fooled. Your task as a parent is to convince your son that he was not a willing accomplice, and that he is not to blame for being sexually violated. He needs to know that he is not at fault for being betrayed and abused, and that it is now safe for him to talk about what has happened.

In order to help you to create a climate that promotes your son's recovery, it is important to review several key points.

- Because sexual predators subtly prepare young victims over time, use of extreme physical force to secure compliance is rare. Tricking a victim with bribes and shows of "apparent kindness" is common. The more inexperienced and minimal the target's social skills, the more he is likely to accept the predator's "generosity" and "friendship" as love and kind affection. Nevertheless, the *threat* of violence is usually made clear once the sexual abuse begins. The predator makes direct or *implied* threats of violence toward the victim or persons that the victim loves in order to secure secrecy. This is one reason why victims are usually fearful to reveal what has happened to them. In addition, if the victim is gay or bisexual, the threat of having his sexual identity made public (i.e., being "outed") by the perpetrator also functions to secure his silence.

- Because betrayal of trust knows no boundaries, sex crimes can be committed by persons of any age, race, religion, profession, or economic group. Perhaps the worst betrayal, however, occurs when the perpetrator is someone the family knows and trusts. The divided loyalties that result from such a betrayal, particularly if the perpetrator is a relative, are like a shock wave that sweeps through the entire family. Nevertheless, the response should be clear: whatever it takes to help your son to recover must come first. Other concerns raised by the perpetrator's place in the family must wait. Even if some family members feel a need to "take sides," your duty is to unequivocally support your child and denounce the perpetrator's actions.

- Despite what some people may believe, young males who are sexually victimized do not invite the assault simply because they may have engaged in risky behaviors. Such a mistaken belief is more likely if the victim is a teenager. Whether the victim engaged in drinking, hitchhiking, running away from home, experimenting with illicit drugs, skipping school, or staying out late, he is not responsible for the perpetrator's actions. Nevertheless, because the victim fears his parents' anger over such behaviors when a sexual assault occurs, he is less willing to reveal what has happened. Often the difficulties of communication between the male victim and his parents are rooted in conflicts over such risky behaviors, which distracts everyone from the central issue: the sexual victimization of the son. The shroud of secrecy and poor communication can be removed only if your son believes that whatever problem behaviors may have occurred before the assault, your first concern is for him as he struggles to recover.

- Male victims may show a range of responses after a sexual assault. Given that young males in our society tend to be socialized to hide their feelings and not to show emotional vulnerability, a hysterical response to their victimization is rare. Some victims are controlled and stoic, others act out inappropriately. All, however, are deeply affected by the experience. Most have deep fears that they are reluctant to share with anyone, including the fears rooted in explicit sexual flashbacks. As we have mentioned, male victims have fears about their sexual identity, their independence, their reputation among peers, and about being blamed for the rape. These fears are usually most pronounced if the victims were abused repeatedly, rather than during a single incident.

As a parent who has a strong sense of responsibility for the safety of your child, you may experience particularly intense reactions, such as rage and self-blame, if your son is raped. When you first learn of the sexual assault, however, it is absolutely critical that you consider the stresses on your son and do everything you can to reassure him *without losing your control*. A persistent state of intense anger will not let you focus on your son's recovery. The following should be kept in mind:

- The sexual assault may cause him to have exaggerated fears about intimacy. Your son, regardless of his age, needs to know that he is not "tarnished," that his capacity to have close relationships will not be reduced, and that the attack on him was a crime of violence, *not* an expression of affection.

- If your son is an adolescent, the attack may aggravate communication problems that already exist. Do not force your son to talk with you about it, but if he shows a willingness to discuss the assault with you, be prepared to do so. If you avoid talking about the assault, it may give your son the impression that you are ashamed and hold him responsible. If he is unwilling to discuss what happened with you, then it is important to make sure that a profes-

50

sional who is trained in child sexual victimization be available to provide assistance.

- Young male victims of sexual violence usually have significant confusion about their sexual identity. Such confusion is seldom something that male victims want to discuss with their parents. Honor that need and help your son select sympathetic and knowledgeable persons who can respond appropriately to his sexual concerns.

- Work to dispel his feelings of shame, embarrassment, and fear. Part of his hidden concerns may be based upon his having persistent and unwanted sexual thoughts that stem from the rape. Very likely, he is ashamed and afraid to say anything to you about these intrusive thoughts. Do not force him to tell you the details of such thoughts. As a parent, you can help by acknowledging that these thoughts are relatively common after an assault and do not mean that he is crazy, perverted, or sexually "changed." By helping him to understand that graphic sexual thoughts may occur when one has been victimized and by giving him permission to talk to you or a to trained professional about these thoughts, you will help to ease some of his most profound concerns.

- Many young male victims are sexually assaulted by their peers. Such assaults often are the extreme expression of a wider pattern of bullying and harassment by peers that has gone unreported. If this is the case, your son may fear that you think he is weak for not having "stood up" to the person or persons who harmed him. He may fear that you will be critical of him for not seeking help to end the harassment. Again, he needs your reassurances that he is not blamed for his conduct, and that he has your unconditional support.

- If your son was assaulted by someone he knows, he may fear you think that he used poor judgment, particularly if he is an adolescent. He also may fear that you will punish him or restrict his freedom. He needs to know that you believe him, that you do not second-guess his judgment, and that there will be no unnecessary restriction of his activities. The latter is especially important. Restricting his activities will reinforce his doubts about his judgment and whether you believe him, which could complicate the communication between you.

- Encourage your son to resume a normal lifestyle, such as playing sports and seeing friends. As noted earlier, restricting him or "grounding" him for not "choosing more carefully" will seem like punishment and could cause resentment. It also is important that he continue his involvement in extracurricular events at school and his responsibilities at home. Being overly protective of him will make his adjustment more difficult.

- A decline in school performance may occur after the revelation that your son was sexually victimized. As a parent, you must strike a balance between making sure that he performs well as a student, while you help him to work through all of the emotional complications associated with rape. If there are academic difficulties, it is appropriate to consult with the school counselor, who is trained to handle such situations. In this case, the need to respect confidentiality must be tempered with the need to facilitate your son's academic success. Sharing information with selected school personnel on a "need to know" basis is a reasonable course of action. Teachers and school counselors are in a position to modify academic tasks and provide support in ways that can aid your son's recovery. If you do consult with school personnel, however, you should tell your son and explain the reasons why.

- Do not isolate yourself or your son from friends who are aware of the rape. Doing so will underscore his belief that he has been diminished in his worth as a person or dishonored as a result of the attack. Remind him (and yourself) that neither of you is to blame for the attack, and that neither of you should feel shame.

- A significant concern of young males who are sexually assaulted is that they will become the object of gossip and ridicule by peers. Male peers especially are inclined to make inappropriate and hurtful remarks about the victim's sexual orientation or "manhood." Although it may be impossible to control all such insensitive remarks by peers, you can teach your son ways to cope with them. Discuss words and actions that will help him to respond effectively to gossip or ridicule. If appropriate, it may help to discuss the assault with his teachers so that they too can be alert to the behavior of his peers. Educators may take the opportunity to educate these students about the consequences of sexual violence and the importance of supporting those who are victims.

- If your son is young, he may show signs of distress through a change in behavior, rather than by articulating what is bothering him. Behavioral reactions in young children are common and should be monitored closely for frequency and severity. Be alert for the following signs:
  - loss of appetite
  - withdrawal
  - altered sleeping patterns or nightmares
  - fear of being alone
  - fear of being touched
  - fear of undressing
  - fear of other people

- bed wetting
- wanting to hide
- excessive crying
- preoccupation with sexual themes in the course of play or conversation

- As we have discussed, it is also common for victims of any age to have flashbacks. For a young victim, however, such flashbacks can cause him to seem almost "frozen" in a horrible moment and thus not be very responsive to the immediate environment. The terrible mental images during a flashback literally take control of the victim's mind, which compounds his mental and emotional turmoil. As a parent, you may be able to help your son regain his grounding in the present by adjusting his attention through *sight, hearing, or touch*. Looking at a comforting photograph, or listening to tranquil music, or touching something safe and familiar, such as a stuffed animal, can diminish the flashback and help him to reestablish equilibrium. The important thing is to direct his senses to that which is safe and familiar, and to do so in a way that makes him feel he has regained some control.

- If the crime is reported to the authorities and the victim is a minor, parental permission may be required for medical treatment and for police questioning. Be available and ready to provide such authorizations and to ensure that official procedures are conducted with sensitivity. Remember, a child is less frightened by accurate information because it gives him a sense of security. Fear of the unknown is usually worse than fear of the known. Avoid springing any surprises on your son, even if you think the action is for the good.

- The medical exam may be physically invasive and extremely upsetting, even if parents and medical staff are sensitive. Gently and firmly convince your son that the procedure is necessary and insist that the medical staff conduct the exam carefully and compassionately. Be sure that every step in the process is clearly explained to your son. If it is appropriate and your son desires the support, you or a trusted person may be present during the exam. If this is not possible, reassure your son by telling him where you will be waiting.

- Monitor older children and adolescents for the consumption of drugs and alcohol. Among those who are already prone to experiment with drugs or alcohol, there may be a sharp increase in substance abuse after the assault. If you are aware that your son is using drugs or alcohol, it is important that you consult with professionals who know how to deal with both the substance abuse and the rape victimization.

- Do not let your son use his victimization to manipulate you inappropriately. Although your son's routine activities will be disrupted for a time, his responsibilities for school, household tasks, or extracurricular activities should not become points of negotiation. He needs to know that, even as you love him and support him as he recovers, you are consistent in your role as his parent.

In providing support for you son, we recognize the difficulty of asking you to subdue your intense feelings and to place his recovery needs first. It is likely that you too will experience anger, rage, disbelief, frustration, protectiveness, grief, and deep sadness. These intense feelings are normal. While it is important not to let your feelings interfere with his recovery, it is also important that you find a constructive way to address your needs. We encourage you to seek a trusted and supportive person with whom you can discuss what you are going through. We believe that an important step in gaining control over powerful and often conflicting emotions is to articulate them to someone who understands.

There are no magic ways for you to make everything right for your son. The most important message is simple: *you love him no matter what*. That message is the basis for keeping open the line of communication, an essential element in his recovery. As a parent, you can hasten your son's recovery by believing his explanation of what happened, and reassuring him that you believe it by communicating openly and honestly, by being nonjudgmental, by not trying to overprotect him, and by demonstrating your unconditional love and consistent support. The dividend for such love and support is earned trust and the knowledge that you have given him the solid foundation upon which he can build a successful recovery.

# 9

# Family and Friends of Incarcerated Victims

Same-sex rape occurs more frequently in prisons and jails than in any other setting. With nearly 2 *million* people in adult jails and prisons in the United States, we know that thousands of rapes take place behind bars each year. Rape in juvenile detention centers also occurs, but there are few published studies on this phenomenon. Because there is no way at present to accurately report these rapes, and because prisoners are at serious risk from other prisoners if they divulge their victimization, we simply do not know the true magnitude of the problem. Yet we can say that for a male who is sexually assaulted in jail or prison, the psychological, social, and sexual effects of the rape are especially horrific.

Prison is a closed, predatory society, in which rape is "normalized." This means that inmates and prison officials alike view rape as an inevitable feature of prison life. Large numbers of male inmates, living in tense and crowded conditions, are continually challenged by "masculinity tests." Deprived of normal means to exhibit their masculinity, some resort to sexual violence as one way to demonstrate their "manhood," to induce fear, and to control other inmates.

When an inmate first arrives in prison, his physical power and his power to control his immediate environment will be tested in many ways. Any perceived weakness will be exploited. Fundamentally, he must decide to risk injury or death through self-defense, or submit to various invasions, including sexual assaults. His decision to fight or to submit will follow him throughout his incarceration.

The prison hierarchy is based upon a limited view of masculine power, with the physically weak at the bottom of this hierarchy. The only "protection" the most vulnerable inmates are given by prison officials is placement in "protective custody" . . . or what other inmates sarcastically refer to as "Punk City." Living in protective custody usually means that the inmates receive fewer privileges than other inmates (e.g., access to recreational facilities; time outside of the cell), are stigmatized within the inmate hierarchy, and face great risk if other inmates gain access to those so confined. Simply stated, for those most vulnerable to sexual assault in prison, few desirable options exist to avoid repeated physical and sexual abuse.

Unfortunately, there seldom are negative consequences for those inmates who prey upon other inmates. All predators in prison, including sexual predators, hold sacred their power within the inmate hierarchy. They are often supported and protected by like-minded gangs who enable them to rape and rape again. Seldom do prison officials detect these attacks. Sometimes prison guards simply turn their backs when an assault takes place. Inmates who are the targets of sexual violence know that they cannot escape and that no one is likely to help them.

How does this happen? Even a rudimentary understanding of prison culture provides insight. In prison culture, there is a gap between appearance and reality. That which appears to be an orderly and controlled environment on the surface does not reflect the constant tension that is present for inmates. Prisoners always have to be vigilant and "watch their backs" because violence, including sexual violence, could happen at any time. Furthermore, the reality of the prison culture means that what is unacceptable conduct outside the prison is acceptable (even commonplace) within. Worse, unacceptable conduct is ignored by outsiders because it takes place within the prison, a place that is intended to be unpleasant. In such an "anything goes" environment, the strong rule with impunity and the weak become targets.

To sexual predators in prison, new and vulnerable inmates are seen as "fresh meat." These new inmates know they are in a helpless position. More powerful and experienced inmates will offer "friendship" and "protection" with strings attached. One goal is to force the new inmate to be sexually available to the person(s) offering protection.

The reality of prison culture is clear: incarcerated victims of sexual violence live in a *continued state of preimpact terror*. Unlike other victims whose preimpact terror is a one-time event, prisoners who are preyed upon by other prisoners experience this terror almost daily. They seldom feel safe. In addition, this terror is induced *intentionally* rather than by accident. The places where people on the outside feel safest — at home, in the shower, at play, or while asleep — are the places where inmates are most vulnerable. There is no respite. In the confines of the prison, victims and predators see one another daily. Even guards and other prison staff, not just fellow prisoners, can be perpetrators. Equally important, if rape victims retaliate against their predators, they risk death by other prisoners, or solitary confinement and more prison time for their conduct. Self-defensive violence by inmates is accorded little consideration by prison officials. For rape victims, retaliation produces more abuse, more prison time, and fewer privileges. The preimpact terror experienced by victims eventually gives way to a simmering silent rage.

Once sexually assaulted by inmates, the victim's status in the inmate hierarchy is reduced to "punk," "kid," "junior" or "catcher," and his risk for subsequent assaults increases. The sexual predators may be called "daddies," "jockers," "wolves," "studs," or "pitchers." Whatever the prison lingo, the predators do not see themselves as homosexuals, even though their targets are

59

other men. In a sense, they attempt to "feminize" their victims by using the threat of violence to impose a "female role" on those who are sexually assaulted. For the predator, there is a double victory: his power is made obvious within the prison hierarchy, and he has a "kid" who is sexually available to him . . . or to other inmates who wish to buy his "kid."

The victimized inmate may weigh the costs of reporting. He is likely to ask himself the following questions: Will I be discovered if I snitch? Do I want my manhood and sexuality questioned? Will I be condemned by my family and friends? Will I be put into protective custody permanently? What do I gain in this system if I report? Will I be killed? Am I a coward if I snitch? In pondering such questions, the victim usually comes to the conclusion that he has little choice but to remain silent.

For the victim, the fear of repeated gang rape usually is sufficient to persuade him to pair off with one predator instead of many. This "decision," however, is not voluntary. It is imposed upon him by a basic reality: this is what he *must* do in order to survive. In offering protection against the physical and sexual violence of other inmates, the predator may even make a show of "kindness" toward the victim. Protection, bribes, and flattery may seem like "kindness," but they are only part of a con game to break down the victim's resistance. The appearance of kindness and the reality of incredible intimidation through the constant threat of violence take their toll. The victim blames himself, questions his sexual identity, sees no way out of his enslavement to other prisoners, feels unable to seek help from prison officials, and can share his pain with no one. The options for victims are few: suicide, acceptance of enslavement, assume the risks of snitching or retaliation, or become a predator by joining with gangs of other predators.

According to the organization Stop Prisoner Rape, the inmates most likely to be the targets of sexual violence when they enter prison are those who are:*

- young or small
- nonviolent and first timers
- middle class
- perceived as homosexual
- not gang-affiliated or street-wise
- not part of a dominant group in the facility
- inexperienced at dealing with physical confrontations
- sentenced to large jails or prisons
- Caucasian
- known to be sentenced for a sex offense

As a friend or loved one, your first concern is for something over which you have little direct control — the inmate's safety. Nevertheless, there are two general categories of things you can do which are helpful: attend to your communications with him and lobby prison officials to respond appropriately to prison rape.

# Communicating with Prisoners

The recommended strategies for effective communication with any male who has been raped also apply to those in prison. Again, sensitivity and trust are essential. To set the stage for helping him, however, it is important that you understand several basic issues of concern facing an inmate who is raped in prison.

- He may be experiencing confused sexual feelings for either sex.

---

*Donaldson, Stephen. *Rape of Incarcerated Males in the U.S.A., A Preliminary Look,* 5th ed., 1994.

- He may have persistent nightmares and disturbing mental images from which he feels unable to escape.

- He may be confused by the attention his "protector" is giving him, especially if he feels that he has been ignored and unloved most of his life.

- He may be worried about his reputation among family and friends.

- He may have fears about contracting a sexually-transmitted infection, including HIV. (Prisons have high-risk populations and will regularly test inmates in order to control diseases.)

- He may have unspoken fears about what he is "becoming" in prison.

With these concerns in mind, we recommend the following to facilitate effective communication with a family member or friend who is an inmate.

- Do not pry into the details of his life behind bars, for it is likely that he is trying to "protect" you from worrying about conditions over which you have no control. Understand that trite expressions, such as "everything is going to be okay," are his way of masking what may be happening.

- Be available to listen, *really* listen to him, for you may be able to detect indirect pleas for help. For example, he may make references to being treated like an animal or "being used and spit out," thus suggesting the possibility of ongoing sexual abuse. Reassure him that whatever he must do to survive, you still view him as a man who possesses dignity.

- Build trust by letting him confide in you on his terms. If he does divulge having been raped, work to dispel his sense of shame. Remind him that no one deserves to be raped, and that despite any doubts he may have about his "manhood," you do not question his sexuality or his male identity.

- Be alert for hints that he may be contemplating suicide. Prisoners who are repeatedly victimized, and who are not likely to be released any time soon, are much more likely to consider suicide as a "way out."

- Provide assurances that your relationship with him has not deteriorated since his incarceration. Do all you can to dispel his fear that you or others who care for him are abandoning him.

- Keep an optimistic and hopeful attitude in all your communications with him throughout his incarceration. Encourage him to focus on positive things over which he does have some control. Often this is his own mental state. For many inmates, the most important battles are the ones they fight in their own heads. Equally important, always encourage him to make good decisions about his life as he anticipates being released. Participation in prison education programs are a good example.

We recognize that as a loved one of an inmate, you carry a substantial emotional burden. At times you probably feel frustration, anger, and possibly fear and hopelessness while you wait for the prisoner's release. You probably ask yourself questions to which there is no clear answer. What will he be like when he is set free? Will he be changed for the worse? What adjustments will you and he have to make? Will the relationship survive? Your concerns and feelings in this regard are understandable. While there are no simple solutions to your legitimate concerns, we believe that you can find comfort in talking to others who are sympathetic and understanding. Whether you confide in a friend, a pastor, a counselor, or a professional who is familiar with prisons, we encourage you to share your emotional burden with someone who is trusted and supportive.

# Communicating with Officials

Until correctional institutions take steps to reduce the risk of sexual assault, many prisoners (especially young ones) will suffer at the hands of a prison culture that defines a clear "pecking order" based upon strength and aggression. One way you can help is to become an advocate for the rights of incarcerated sexual-assault victims, demanding that authorities foster an environment that minimizes the risk of victimization. Prisons have a moral and a legal obligation to protect inmates. Do all you can to hold them accountable to this obligation.

- As an advocate, you can demand that the prison establish a means to monitor the frequency of prisoner rape, and the locations where it is most common. In addition, insist that clear consequences for sexual predators be enacted and enforced (e.g., isolating known perpetrators and imposing on them strict sanctions).

- You could insist that the prison follow the suggestions of reformers that confidential rape counseling be provided to any prisoner requesting it (by therapists who specialize in rape recovery). You may also suggest to state correctional authorities that facilities coordinate with community rape-crisis centers to assist prisoners in their recovery. Unfortunately, however, there is considerable variation in the willingness of prisons and community rape-crisis centers to work together. If community centers are unable or unwilling to accept the challenge of working with incarcerated victims of rape, then it should be the responsibility of corrections officials to provide the needed support services to these inmates.

- Advocate for employee-training programs about rape at correctional facilities. Also, request that all new inmates undergo an orientation that focuses on how to get help and what to do in the event of a sexual assault. Inmates need to know that the prison is responding to a basic need . . . the need to create a safe haven even behind bars. Inmates also need to know that they have a basic right to be free from assault, and that prison officials take this right seriously. Taking this right seriously means that there must be some means to redress inmate grievances, to hold predators accountable for assaults, and to ensure that guards are accountable for inmate safety.

In 1995, the Federal Bureau of Prisons enacted a protocol that requires each federal institution to have programs for inmate education, prevention, screening and classification, staff training, and prompt and effective intervention.* Each state institution should also establish such programs. Until each state facility meets the standards now in place at federal facilities, however, you may seek information from your local rape-crisis center or call the nationwide referral number (800-656-HOPE) to find the center closest to you. You may also contact Stop Prisoner Rape (860) 684-9370 for additional information. Neither you nor the person who is incarcerated needs to stand alone.

---

*Bureau of Presons Program Statement, number 5324.02, February 2, 1995, effective May 1, 1995, U.S. Department of Justice.

# 10
# Finding Help

In most communities, there are several possible sources of help for rape survivors and their support persons, including community mental-health centers, pastoral counseling services, and private practitioners. There are also a number of national organizations dedicated to helping victims and their families.

In addition, hundreds of rape-crisis centers have been established in communities throughout the United States and Canada. These centers specialize in addressing the needs of victims; they provide assistance free of charge. Many also provide services to family members of victims. While some rape-crisis centers only provide services to women, many are willing to help males who are raped. Rape-crisis services for females have progressed over the last two decades and services for male victims are emerging. Do not be discouraged if you reach out and an agency is unprepared to help you. Keep trying. If they cannot provide help, ask them to guide you to someone who can help. Some centers run groups for males and offer them counseling. If no such group is available, encourage the center to start one. Encourage the staff to expand their training to include male rape issues. Virtually all rape-crisis centers will make referrals to help males locate additional services.

As we have mentioned, many males are reluctant to seek help because they believe it is a sign of weakness or because they do not want their sexuality to be questioned. Many will resist discussing their victimization because of their discomfort with the emotional vulnerability associated with receiving help. Even when male rape victims do seek help, they often do so in ways which hide their true purpose for making contact with helpers. For example, some male victims will visit a rape-crisis service on the pretext that they are doing a term paper on rape, or that they want information to help a "friend." Those who provide help should be alert to males who mask their victimization when they initiate contact.

In our culture, males generally are taught to be aggressive, emotionally tough, self-reliant, and independent. These are values that tend to discourage male victims from asking for help or accepting it when it is offered. Because it is difficult for some males to acknowledge their emotional vulnerability, you need to reinforce the message that accepting help in the aftermath of a rape is not an indication of weakness or an admission that he "can't take it." Rather, it is a realization that there are those whose professional training places them in a position to offer guidance at a time of great need. Seeking help is *not* a sign of weakness; it is a sign of intelligence and strength.

The earlier the victim seeks assistance, the better the chance for his timely recovery. Even if the rape took place years before and is just now coming to light, he can still benefit from professional guidance. Still, it is not easy to disclose that one has been raped. A vital element in a victim's decision to seek help comes from assurances that he will not be judged, and that he will be protected if he breaks his silence. In large measure, the courage to break the silence also comes from your support and from his belief that he will be believed. It *is* an act of courage to speak out. Rapists do not want witnesses. They threaten and intimidate their victims into secrecy. They pretend that they did nothing wrong. The perpetrator can say, "It never happened," or "He is lying," or "He got what he asked for." Too often, it is the *victim's* behavior that is questioned. In giving the victim support and encouragement, you are helping to give him a voice.

As he progresses through his recovery, he may even decide to help other rape victims or to work to raise public awareness about rape. As many rape survivors have learned, healing often is aided by extending one's self to help others. Because you are a person who cares about him, and because you are one who is standing by him throughout the ordeal, you can help bring him to a place where the victimization does not control his life, or yours.

# Case Study 1
## Ben: An Adolescent Victim Who is Isolated

Ben had been in the custody of Child Welfare Services for most of his 13 years. Unhappy, Ben often went AWOL from his "home" — the state-run shelter. During one of these unauthorized excursions, Ben wandered alone along a jogging trail where he met a "friendly man" named Ralph who was in his 30s. Ralph seemed to take a true interest in Ben, acting as if he cared about Ben as a person. After establishing rapport, Ben's new acquaintance asked, "Do you like my bike shorts?" When Ben indicated that he did, Ralph said, "I've got an extra pair that'll probably fit you. Let's go to my apartment." Although Ben felt vaguely uncomfortable with the invitation, he trusted Ralph and he wanted the shorts. Needing adult approval and attention, Ben agreed to go home with Ralph.

Once in the apartment, Ralph insisted that Ben try on the shorts so he could see how they fit. Ben's gnawing feeling of uneasiness continued to grow but he did as the man urged. When Ben shyly walked out of the bathroom wearing the shorts, Ralph nodded approvingly. Yawning dramatically, Ralph suggested that they take a nap. Ben was unsure what would happen if he said no, but he felt that Ralph's invitation was not so much a request as it was an order.

Cautiously, Ben sat down on Ralph's bed. Suddenly, Ralph pushed Ben down and fondled his genitals over his shorts. Ben froze. Before Ben knew what hit him, Ralph flipped him over on his stomach, yanked down his prized bike shorts, and anally raped him. The pain was terrible. Ben thrashed about wildly and finally was able to grab the side of the bed.

Then, with an adrenalin rush, he threw Ralph off of him. Ben managed to grab his clothes and stumble out of the apartment. Terror kept him running back to his shelter-home where he wiped the tears from his face but not the red from his eyes.

It was obvious to the child welfare workers that Ben was hurting when he limped in the door. Dorothy, his case manager, called the police when Ben incoherently sobbed, "He attacked me." Dorothy just held Ben and rocked him until the police arrived.

Frightened and confused by the police officer's questions, Ben gave a terse account of what happened. "The guy got me hard in the butt. I hurt real bad." The officer then took Ben to the hospital for a medical exam.

On the way Ben cried in silence. When the nurse examiner gently asked him what had happened, Ben began to feel safe enough to reveal the details. Armed with the truth, the police quickly apprehended Ralph.

The day before Ralph's preliminary hearing Ben spoke with the new assistant district attorney, a young male. Dorothy brought Ben to the courthouse but was unable to stay with him during the interview — she had another case that demanded her attention. Alone in the room with the young attorney, Ben was afraid to tell in his own words what had happened.

The assistant district attorney then became noticeably irritated at Ben's "refusal" to do anything more than nod when asked a question. The prosecutor then said, "As hard as this is, I don't know of anyone who has died from a sexual assault." That remark was cold comfort for Ben. The prosecutor tersely ended the interview with instructions for Ben to be back in the morning for the hearing. "We'll see what happens," the attorney said as he abruptly left for his next appointment.

Ben remained silent at the shelter. None of the case workers inquired of Ben what had happened at the attorney's office. He felt totally isolated and wondered if anyone cared. That night, Ben went AWOL again. With a "no-show" victim, the prosecutor requested that the hearing be postponed for a week. The prosecutor was very upset with Ben. Then, after three additional court post-ponements because Ben continued to avoid the scheduled hearings, the judge ruled in favor of the defense attorney's motion to dismiss the case. After all, Ralph had a constitutional right to a speedy trial, and the principal witness against him "refused" to cooperate.

Several weeks later, a five alarm fire was started on the top floor of a high-rise office complex. After questioning, Ben was arrested and convicted with two other teenage boys for arson. Ben was placed in custody at a maximum security detention center for juvenile delinquents.

## Our Analysis

This case illustrates the critical need for victims to have a support system in the aftermath of a sexual assault. It also points out the problems one may encounter in being assigned to an over-worked social service professional and to a district attorney with limited communication skills. Remember that immediately after the rape, Ben's responses to questions were brief and guarded. It was not until his needs for safety and security were met that Ben disclosed the details of what had happened.

Both Dorothy and the nurse examiner provided some of the initial security and nurturing that Ben needed in order to speak honestly about the rape. Unfortunately, that good start was not sustained. Because Ben had no family, it was crucial that his case worker give him the time and attention he needed. The reality, however, is that case workers usually are so overwhelmed that they seldom have the time to devote intense effort to the needs of any single person. For example, despite her good intentions, Dorothy was unable to be with Ben during his interview with the assistant district attorney. Lack of support at this critical moment set the stage for Ben's inability to face the ordeal of going forth with the prosecution of Ralph.

To make matters worse, the young prosecutor may have known the law, but he was not versed in how to properly interview victims of rape. His thoughtless remark ("Nobody ever died from a sexual assault") and his apparent irritation at Ben's "uncooperative attitude" led to what followed. Without support and sensitivity from those in charge of the investigation, Ben understandably decided to avoid further revictimization by ducking the legal proceedings. He protected himself in the only way he knew how — by choosing the path of least resistance and running from his problems. Ben had reached an intersection. One direction was paved with perceived insensitivity, the other with self-preservation. Ben chose the latter. Perhaps saddest of all, in setting a fire Ben received swift justice as a perpetrator of arson, though he was never afforded justice as a victim of rape.

It is clear that much pain and injustice could have been avoided if Ben had been given the long term support he needed after the rape. The reality is that the heavy case loads and high turnover of social service workers, coupled with the lack of victim interview training among those charged with enforcing the law, increases the likelihood that victims such as Ben will be "uncooperative."

Even victims who have family available to them for support, however, may encounter problems. No system is perfect. Despite good intentions, sooner or later someone is likely to do something that seems callous, thus complicating the recovery of victims. This is all the more reason why rape victims, in the pursuit of justice, should not have to face "the system" alone.

Even though no one can change the fact that Ben was raped, he did not need to feel helpless as he struggled with what had happened. By giving Ben compassion and support, and by providing him with choices and understanding following the assault, this tragic course of events might have been avoided.

## What Would You Do?

What does this mean for caring persons who are not is social services or the legal system? Remember that Ben was a "loner" who felt totally isolated. He had neither family nor friends to support him. But what if Ben was your friend, sibling, or son? What would you do? Clearly Ben's case demonstrates the need for someone, anyone, to reduce his isolation. Alone, Ben was at severe risk of hurting himself, hurting others, or being hurt again by others.

Should a similar situation arise with a young, isolated male rape victim whom you know, the actions you take (or fail to take) could be critical to his recovery — and even to his survival. Perhaps the most fundamental thing you should do is to be certain that he does not go through the trauma alone. Try to provide the kind of support suggested throughout this book. Yet, even if you are never in a position to provide direct support to a male rape victim such as Ben, you can voice your support for more reasonable case loads for social service providers. You also can voice support favoring better training for law enforcement personnel who work with victims of rape. The trauma of rape should never be compounded by the responses of those in human services and the legal profession.

# Case Study 2
# Steve: Homeless and Gang-Raped

Steve, an 18-year-old, had lived for several months with Kevin but decided to leave when Kevin came on to him sexually. Several weeks after Steve left, Kevin found him living under the bridge where they first had met. It was cold and rainy. When Kevin offered to take him back to his warm, dry apartment, Steve agreed. This seemed to be a better alternative than living on the street. Once in the apartment, however, Steve was greeted by two other male strangers. Without warning, they jumped him and bound his wrists and feet together. Steve had been set-up.

The men held Steve's legs straight up and threatened to crush his skull if he failed to cooperate. To reinforce their threat, they punched Steve in the face and clubbed him with a bottle. The attackers then wrapped a chain around his neck. Kevin was aroused as he watched the two attackers take turns anally raping Steve. In excruciating pain, Steve fainted during the assault.

After what seemed like hours, Steve "woke up," saw he was alone, untied himself and fled. Although it was painful to move, he ran to a convenience store and called 911. The dispatcher responded with a sarcastic, "sing-song" tone as he repeated the problem back to Steve.

Clearly, the dispatcher was disbelieving and unsympathetic. When Steve's voice started to quiver, the dispatcher, in a cold monotone voice, asked Steve if he needed an ambulance. The dispatcher seemed annoyed. Steve said, "No! I need the police. I've just been raped by two guys."

There was a long pause followed by a sigh. Then the dispatcher said, "All right, we will send an officer out." Within minutes a police officer arrived, followed by a back-up car. After telling both officers what happened, Steve leaned against the outside wall of the convenience store while he listened to the officers talk about him in front of him.

The second officer, an older man, seemed concerned when he asked Steve if he was all right. Steve wondered if the officer was sincere. "No," Steve said, "I want to die." In a kindly fashion, the officer gently put his hand on Steve's upper arm and nudged him to the side. He then said, "We are going to catch these guys if it's the last thing we do."

Steve took a deep breath for the first time since he was raped. He was glad breathing was "automatic" because it would have required too much effort to do so consciously. His physical injuries throbbed. When he groaned, the first officer suggested he get into the front seat of his patrol car. Steve stared out the window and wondered how he could face the people at the hospital and endure a rape exam. As they approached the hospital entrance Steve felt detached, almost as if he was an observer rather than a participant in some grotesque drama.

At the hospital, the nurse and the rape victim advocate told him what to expect. Steve had not showered in days and felt humiliated when he was asked to take off his soiled jeans and shirt. He stood on a piece of paper which covered the floor. The advocate held up a sheet in front of him while the nurse examined his body for physical injuries. The places where he had been bound had left red marks which the nurse wanted to photograph. Steve flashed back on the moment when his limbs were tied: he knew exactly what was going to happen to him and there was nothing he could do about it. Terror again swept over him. Although he said nothing, the camera's flash documented what would take a lifetime for him to forget.

Sensing his pain, the victim advocate asked him if there was someone he wanted to call in order to be with him. Steve's mind raced. He was embarrassed because he knew no one whom he could call — no one he trusted enough to share his humiliation. If his family saw him unshaven, unbathed, and now raped, it would just confirm their disgust with him, he reasoned. "I want to handle this by myself," he whispered.

After the exam, the police asked to him come down to the precinct station to view a line-up. They had apprehended Kevin and one of the two strangers. Steve was told that he needed to positively identify them. He froze as he remembered what he just endured. "I just can't," he said adamantly.

The victim advocate led him to a small, private consultation room where Steve shared his fear that he would be killed if he helped prosecute the rapists. "Plus," he added, "The other guy hasn't been caught. When I go back to the bridge, I know he will find me." Together they considered options and then Steve was tentatively convinced that cooperating with the police would give him more protection than hiding-out. Steve agreed to stay at a shelter for up to four weeks for protection.

While staying at the shelter, Steve received counseling. He still did not talk with his family. But after several counseling sessions, Steve began to turn his anger into positive life decisions. Eventually he found work and realized, "I think I am going to be able to smile at my future . . . once again."

Not only did Steve help himself, but he became active in a male peer-support group. With the help of the group, the stigma of his experience was lessened by the realization that other men also have been raped. Steve began to heal as he helped others. He participated in the group for two years, showing that male victims do not have to be alone in their recovery.

## What Would You Do?

What can we learn from Steve's case? Perhaps the most important lesson is that Steve received immediate help from a rape crisis advocate and from others. This initial assistance then was augmented by group support over time. Even though he was homeless and without the support of his family, those who helped Steve correctly approached him in a nonjudgmental, patient, and tolerant manner. He also was placed in an environment where he felt safe. These are powerful actions that aid in the recovery process.

If you are a friend of a male rape victim who is alienated from his family, follow the example above: be approachable, tolerant, nonjudgmental, and patient. Help to create a feeling of safety where the victim can share his pain and feel accepted. Reinforce the message that he is not responsible for being raped. These actions on your part will help to set the tone for his recovery.

It also is important for you to help the victim to understand that professional assistance is available in the community. Learn what you need to know about rape crisis services in order to explain to him his options. Give him information and choices so that he may begin to regain a sense of control over his life. Also, be a good listener and affirm his courage for his willingness to talk about being the victim of rape.

Whether you are a family member, friend, or public servant who first responds to a male rape victim, there is a crucial need to listen without judgment. In so doing, you will be creating a climate where he feels secure and can asked for and receive the help he needs.

There is one final point to consider when communicating with male victims of rape. It is important to affirm to the victim that same-sex rape is not a consensual sex act between gay men. Rape is never consensual and homophobic reactions by others will only complicate the victim's recovery.

Professionals, as well as family and friends, can do much to restore a victim's equilibrium through dispelling blame and rejecting the homophobic misconceptions associated with same-sex rape.

# Case Study 3
# Tim: An Adolescent Molested
# by His Stepfather

Tim did not feel isolated when his parents divorced. Most of his friends were in the same boat. The custody issue was resolved quickly; everyone, including Tim, agreed he should live with his mother. Unfortunately, his father moved out of state, thus placing great physical and emotional distance between them.

Tim's mother remarried several years later. At the time of the assault, Tim was fourteen and his stepfather was in his 30s. Tim liked his stepfather because he was youthful and seemed to understand him. They often talked, especially when his mother was away on business. Tim was used to her traveling and enjoyed the extra freedom he seemed to have when his mother was away.

On a weekday evening when his mother was traveling, his stepfather offered Tim a drink of whiskey after dinner. Wanting to demonstrate how "grown-up" he was, Tim accepted the drink. They watched television together and had several more drinks. Tim felt light-headed. Although he had tasted alcohol a few times, he had never before consumed this much.

While on the couch, the stepfather placed his arm around Tim and told him how much he cared about him. Although Tim felt close to his stepfather, there was something about this display of affection that did not seem right. As the stepfather hugged him, he said he wanted Tim to know how much he cared about him. Tim's stepfather also said that he wanted to show him a "secret way" in which men who care about each other can be close.

The stepfather then reached down and began to fondle Tim. Tim froze, unsure what his stepfather was doing. Tim had never had a sexual encounter of any kind, and certainly had no experience with anything remotely like this. Tim's stepfather continued to fondle him until Tim got an erection. He also exposed himself as he fondled Tim. Eventually, Tim ejaculated. Throughout, Tim never spoke or moved.

The next morning, Tim could not even look at his stepfather. He was confused, afraid, and hurt. He also felt terribly guilty. Tim kept flashing on the images of what had happened. From that point on, Tim avoided his stepfather.

For days Tim tried to pretend that "it really didn't happen," but when he was with his friends, he dropped hints about it. One of his friends picked up the hint and told the school counselor. When asked directly by the counselor, Tim broke down and cried. He told everything. Child protective services was called and the police were notified.

Tim's mother was in shock and disbelief when the investigator talked with her. She said, "Do you mean to tell me that my son and my husband got drunk and got it on?" She was extremely upset and seemed angry at both of them. She agreed that for the time being, it would be best if Tim were brought to a shelter until she could "sort this out" with her husband.

While at the shelter, Tim's biological father flew out to be with him for a few days. Unfortunately, Tim's father was not able to take Tim back home with him. He left behind a thoroughly traumatized son and an ex-wife apparently headed for another divorce.

After spending two weeks at the shelter, Tim returned home. His mother had decided to divorce her husband, who was now under court order to keep his distance from Tim. Sadly, Tim's mother seemed unable to address Tim's needs for comfort and reassurance, while also processing her own grief.

There seemed to be a looming silence about the matter that neither knew how to overcome. Although she never said as much, Tim felt as if he was being blamed for his mother and stepfather breaking up. He also felt responsible for the legal difficulties now facing his stepfather. And throughout, the terrible images of that night remained with him. Tim became sullen and withdrawn; at times he felt that as though he wanted to die.

Tim's mother recognized that both she and her son were not doing well. In a well-intended effort to improve the situation, she called a minister and asked if he would talk to Tim. Tim was told of the appointment after it was already set. Tim interpreted this as an indication that his mother believed he had committed a terrible sin, and he refused to go. Tim's refusal only complicated communication with his mother. Emotionally distraught, Tim began acting out inappropriately. He was keeping alcohol in his locker at school and drinking it between classes. He was disciplined several times for fights at school. He was having nasty arguments with his mother.

Finally, Tim's mother sought professional guidance. She told Tim that she loved him and proposed that they both enter a counseling program with a therapist who specialized in incest cases. This became a turning point.

Both began to talk about the pain, the loss, and the deeply confusing feelings caused by the actions of Tim's stepfather. Tim and his mother eventually were able to forge a new bond based on a deeper understanding of each other. They came to realize how each had been victimized, though not in the same way. From that point on, their relationship began to heal.

## Our Analysis

One thing about Tim's case is obvious: incest produces great pain, confusion, and divided loyalties within a family. In particular, this case illustrates the special problems facing the mate of a family member who is a perpetrator and the complications this poses for the child. With incest, being violated sexually is uniquely traumatic because the perpetrator is a family member who is loved and trusted. Inevitably, families are ripped apart in the aftermath of an incest disclosure. Family members take sides, blame each other, blame themselves, and feel terrible about the legal consequences for the perpetrator. It is certain that family relationships will never be quite the same in the wake of incest. Everyone is harmed.

The other thing that is obvious about this case is that family members can seldom resolve the deep conflicts produced by incest if they fail to communicate honestly with one another. In the absence of communication, the wound festers without relief. Although it is very difficult to talk about sexual abuse within the family, remaining silent about incest usually results in conflict, growing resentment, mutual distrust, and the inability to be supportive of one another in times of need. Incest is not something that can be ignored in the hope that everything will be resolved over time.

## What Would You Do?

Tim's case illustrates that the most important thing you must do is to think about the needs of both victims. The needs of the child who has been victimized must be given priority, but you also must consider the needs of the non-offending mother. This is because the non-offending mother will play a significant role in the extent to which her child will recover from the assault. The likelihood is considerable that unless she too receives help she will inadvertently make matters worse. The first message to all parties, and particularly to the victim, is that it was not his fault that he was sexually abused. He is not responsible for any family conflict that ensues in the wake of incest disclosure. In the particular case of Tim, he is not responsible for causing his parents to divorce or for his stepfather being incarcerated. When a parent or stepparent is the perpetrator of sexual abuse, it is especially important that the non-offending parent relieve her or his child of any responsibility.

The other message you should give to family members is that not just the victim, but the family as a unit, needs to find a way to communicate about the abuse and its consequences. Unfortunately, it is common for the loved ones of an incest victim to think that "only the person attacked needs help." The greatest help for victims occurs when all members of the family work together to heal. Such healing will not take place in a climate of silence and blame.

# Case Study 4
# Larry: An Inmate Who Was Raped

It was his first time in prison. He had arrived at the facility nine months earlier and was scheduled to serve a four-year sentence for a drug-related crime. Larry, age 20, was short, frail, Caucasian, and not streetwise. From the moment he arrived, the other inmates saw that Larry had "target" written all over him.

"He called me punk and said he was going to make me his woman," Larry whispered as he sat with his head hung low. A thick silver chain was doubled wrapped around his waist; his wrists were shackled in an awkward position. One of the guards who transported Larry to the rape exam site smiled as he spoke to the person conducting the rape exam. "Not every prison handcuffs its inmates this way. We do it to reduce the number of complaints filed. Even though the prisoners find it uncomfortable, it saves us paperwork."

Larry had been taken into a private exam area. An older male rape crisis advocate was called to assist during the invasive exam. Meanwhile, a female advocate talked with the officers who brought Larry in for treatment. She wanted to assess his safety for when he returned to prison. She listened carefully as the guards talked freely about conditions "at work."

The guards said they were tired of "inmates' rights." Too many prisoners file too many complaints over "every little thing." The officers argued that it becomes a nuisance and a waste of time processing these "frivolous" grievances. To reduce such complaints, the prison put in place a new system. Now, when a prisoner reports any form of abuse, he has to name and confront the perpetrator before he is put into protective custody. "Used to be we just put them in P.C. when their life was in danger without our finding out who was threatening them. Now we make them face the person. It sure has reduced a lot of complaints."

The female advocate asked three questions. "Did Larry have to disclose the perpetrator's name before he was brought in for the rape exam? Did he have to confront the person or persons who did this? Is his life now in danger?"

One of the guards looked at her and said, "These guys in prison kill over a cheeseburger. Nobody's safe."

Meanwhile Larry was in an adjoining room undergoing a medical exam. "Is this the first time you were assaulted?" the sexual assault examiner asked Larry while observing massive scarring.

"Yes" he replied untruthfully. When asked who had done this to him, Larry refused to answer. He said, "If you snitch, you die. All I know is that I couldn't take it anymore. That's why I tried to escape."

The female rape advocate who had talked with the guards was invited into a consultation area to speak with Larry before he returned to lock-up.

"Are you worried about going back?" she asked.

"They'll put me in lock-up for a while. They always do that when someone tries to escape. Everybody knows by now that I came here to get my butt examined. If they think that I snitched, they'll make me pay. Even if they transfer me somewhere else, the guys will know before I get there."

The advocate felt helpless. She dreaded the thought of the danger Larry would face. The inmates, the officers, the entire system seemed to work against Larry. "Would you be willing to talk to a prison chaplain if you needed help?" she asked. Larry shrugged his shoulders but said nothing.

"Larry," the advocate continued, "I know I don't understand all you have been through. But I care. I have met the chaplain at your facility. He knows what goes on. I know he will help."

The officers came into the room and again wrapped the thick chain around him. His wrists were cuffed and his ankles were chained together. Larry looked terrified as he shuffled out the door. Once back in the cell block, Larry thought it would be more prudent if he never said anything to the chaplain or anyone else about what had happened. In fact, Larry never "snitched" on who had raped him. He never divulged that he had been raped multiple times, and that he would continue to be sexually violated throughout his prison stay.

When Larry finally was released following the completion of his sentence he seemed to be a broken man. He did not want to discuss anything about his time in prison with his family or friends. He was withdrawn, angry, depressed, and distrustful even of those who cared about him. He began to drink heavily, though he risked violating his parole. Once, when he was drunk, he uttered "I'm not a man anymore. I just want to die."

## Our Analysis

Larry's case is typical of many inmates who are sexually assaulted in prison. He has few choices in a brutal system that fails to prevent rape, and fails to protect those who divulge rape. In such a system the difficulty of helping rape victims to recover is extremely difficult. It is equally difficult for family and friends to act in ways that will reduce the immediate risks for loved ones who are incarcerated.

The depth of Larry's hopelessness is shown by his escape attempt and by the very act of reporting his rape. What did he have to lose? Since both an escape or a reported rape could get him killed, Larry may have even had a death wish. Anything may have seemed better than continuing to be raped with no hope of escape from his torment.

The enormity of the problem of prison rape seems overwhelming. Ideally, prison officials should organize a rape reduction program that monitors sexual assaults and holds rapists accountable. The prison also should make rape crisis intervention a standard part of services available to inmates. A protocol of mandatory training, perhaps coordinated through health services staff, should be standard for all correctional services personnel. When such a protocol is in place, a system of accountability needs to ensure that all correctional staff follow appropriate procedures when they learn of a sexual assault.

An example of such a protocol is the U.S. Department of Justice Sexual Assault Prevention/Intervention Program for inmates incarcerated in federal institutions. This protocol includes the following: 1) screening inmates within 24 hours of admission to determine their vulnerability; 2) a program coordinator to train staff to recognize the signs of sexual assault among inmates; 3) periodic review of reporting procedures; 4) staff training in rape prevention and response techniques. Yearly reports then are filed with a regional administrator who tracks sexual assault.

By monitoring and evaluating sexual assault levels, an institution becomes not only more responsible in reducing prisoner rape, but it also becomes more accountable through a standard developed nationally. State run and privately run penal institutions need to look at the Bureau of Prison's protocol and adapt appropriate measures.

## What Would You Do?

At the least, you can encourage the prison to adopt the guidelines mentioned above. While a loved one is in prison, however, the reality is that there is little you can do to directly alter the threat he faces every day. Perhaps the best you can do is to listen to him, show your support, and encourage him to act in ways that will increase his timely release. You should not demand that he tell you whether he is the victim of sexual violence. If he does divulge being a victim, however, follow the guidelines for communicating with him outlined in this book.

The time when family members and friends usually can be most helpful to an inmate's recovery is after his release. The gradual process of building trust and of creating a climate of support should be your focus.

Remember that it is normal for him to be reluctant to discuss a pattern of sexual victimization while in prison. It is normal for him to have intense feelings of anger, distrust, resentment, and self-blame. It is normal for him to have concerns about his sexuality, and to have concerns about how others might stigmatize him. What you can do to help is to articulate your awareness that such concerns are indeed normal and understandable. It is also important that you confirm to him that he is capable of coming to terms with all of the terrible experiences encountered during his prison stay.

In Larry's case, the depression and the anger are corrosive. Without help, he may strike out at others, or he may turn his anger inward and become suicidal. It is very important that professional guidance be available to him. If he refuses such help, you may be able to place him in contact with self-help groups of former inmates. Released prisoners may be more willing to talk with those who have survived prison than with "outsiders" who they believe may never understand. It is our firm belief that being able to talk about being the victim of rape in prison is a positive step toward regaining control and toward rebuilding trust in others.

# Case Study 5
# Taylor: A Child Molested by a Neighbor

Taylor, a child of six, "helped" his Mom babysit Rodney, a 12-year-old boy who lived next door. Sally, Taylor's Mom, was single and supplemented her minimum-wage job by helping to care for other children. Of all the extra jobs Sally had, this was Taylor's favorite because Rodney let Taylor play on his computer. Sally could not foresee a problem when Taylor and Rodney played together.

Yet one day she felt a gnawing apprehension over the lack of noise in the bedroom where the children were playing. When she tiptoed to the room, she saw Rodney's head on Taylor's genital area. She screamed at them and Taylor started to cry. Rodney immediately jumped off Taylor and darted out of the house. He stayed at the swing set in the backyard until the police arrived.

Taylor told the police they were just playing "no hands." He said, "Rodney pulled down his pants and put a candy bar 'down there' and told me to get it without using my hands. I tried to bite it but it kept moving. So, Rodney held my head down. Then he told me it was my turn. Rodney put the candy 'down there' and started kissing me. He said it was part of no hands."

When Taylor was taken back into the bedroom by the police, he started to cry. His mom pointed a finger at the officer's chest and said, "This may be a routine report for you but it is not for me." He looked at her and said softly, "It's not routine for me either." As the officer questioned him, Taylor continued to cry every time he spoke. Despite the officer's attempts to assure him that he did nothing wrong, Taylor remained agitated. The officer stopped and said, "Would you like to ride in my car to the hospital so we can do an exam?" Taylor agreed and asked if he could hear the siren blast. At the hospital, Sally became even more upset when the officer said, "I doubt if anything will be done about this because of Rodney's age." Several days later, Rodney's mother talked with Sally. She said she thought that Rodney may have also been molested by someone and that Rodney, not Taylor, was the real victim. Shortly thereafter, Rodney's family started intimidating Sally so that she would take no action against Rodney. One evening, Sally saw someone in the front yard. When she stepped outside, she discovered bullets with her initials and Taylor's initials pasted on them. The police canvassed the neighborhood and several of the neighbors identified Rodney's uncle as the person who placed the bullets in the yard. The assistant district attorney in charge of the case was furious. Unfortunately, however, the neighbors who identified Rodney's uncle recanted their statements because they now feared for their own safety.

Sally kept Taylor inside the house most of the time. He seemed startled whenever the phone rang or someone came to the door. Feeling isolated from her neighbors and weary of the court process, Sally plummeted into a deep depression. She was unable to work. During this time, she and Taylor were referred for counseling at a center specializing in male child sexual abuse. Sally's ability to express her concerns and to support Taylor improved. They began to do fun activities together. She consistently reinforced the message that Taylor was not to blame for what had happened.

The juvenile court charged Rodney with lewd molestation and placed him on probation for six months. Rodney was required to be in school everyday and to stay out of trouble. If he completed probation without getting into trouble, the charge would be dropped and the criminal history sealed.

The court also ordered that Rodney receive counseling. Sally thought that the punishment was too lenient, but she felt better knowing that if Rodney did anything to violate the conditions of his probation, he would be placed in a secure facility.

## Our Analysis

In this case, Sally felt guilty for not protecting her son from Rodney and angry at the perpetrator. Such feelings are common among parents when a child is harmed. Yet neither self-blame nor festering anger will help the child. Fortunately, Sally sought help for herself and for Taylor. By reassuring Taylor that he was not to blame and by sharing fun activities with him, she gradually restored a healthy home climate for both of them.

Sally also advocated for her son so that he would be treated with compassion and fairness in the criminal justice system. Rodney was released back into the community, but Sally took some comfort in knowing that he had to meet strict probationary conditions. Her concerns about his revictimizing Taylor (or other children) were balanced by the realization that if Rodney stepped out of line, he would be locked up.

Although she may have preferred a harsher consequence, she accepted the court's decision. Complaining about a decision over which she had no control would help neither her nor her son. Her advocacy for Taylor was best served by her willingness to voice her opinion yet accept the judge's ruling.

## What Would You Do?

While a parent's response will depend in part on the nature and circumstances of the crime, it is correct to report the assault to the authorities. Reporting protects the victim by controlling the perpetrator and by marshaling resources for healing. It also protects others who might become victims if the perpetrator remains undetected. Despite the need to report, however, we recognize that legal processes do not always work in ways which victims and their families find acceptable. Even so, a parent's distress over legal responses following the assault of a child should not be made obvious to that child. Constant expressions of anger and frustration toward the legal system may increase the child's fears and sense of guilt.

The child's need to feel safe and free of blame should dictate the parent's response. Parents also should be alert to the emergence of atypical behaviors in the child. Fear of people, nightmares, bed wetting, loss of appetite, and exaggerated startle responses are examples. If such behaviors emerge, it is important to seek professional guidance. If your son has flashbacks, you can help to adjust his attention through sight, hearing and touch as recommended in this book. This includes directing his attention to something close at hand that is safe and familiar in order to reestablish his sense of control.

When violent or threatening events occur, children take their cues from their parents as to the appropriate response. Remember that a violent, explosive reaction on your part will only harm your child's recovery.

Also, be careful not to "overprotect" your son by isolating him. He may view your well-intended response as punishment or blame for the assault. Consistently remind him that he is not to blame, and remember also that neither are you.

# Resources

**American Correctional Association**
(Handles correctional facility grievances.)
4380 Forbes Blvd.
Lanham, MD 20706
Phone: 800-ACA-JOIN
Web Site: www.corrections.org.aca

**Centers for Disease Control**
National AIDS Hotline
P.O. Box 13827
Research Triangle Park, NC 27709
800-342-AIDS
800-344-SIDA (Spanish)
Web Site: www.ashastd.org

**Childhelp USA**
15757 N. 78 St.
Scottsdale, AZ 85260
1-800-4-A-CHILD

**Gays and Lesbians Opposing Violence (GLOV)**
(Reports taken for hate crimes and harassment.)
Washington, DC
202-737-4568

**Men's Resource Center**
(Offender treatment)
12 SE 14th
Portland, OR 97214
503-215-7082 Hotline
503-235-3433 Telephone

**National AIDS Clearinghouse**
Centers for Disease Control
(Prevention and technical assistance)
P.O. Box 6003
Rockville, MD 20849
800-458-5231
800-243-7012 (TDD)
Web Site: www.cdcnac.org

**National Clearinghouse on Child Sexual Abuse and Neglect**
P.O. Box 1182
Washington, DC 20013
800-394-3366
www.calib.com/nccanch

**National Coalition Against Sexual Assault**
125 Enola Drive
Enola, PA 17025
717-728-9764

**National Crime Victims Center**
Medical University of South Carolina
171 Ashley Avenue
Charleston, SC 29425
803-792-2945
www.mvsc.edu/cvc

**National Gay and Lesbian Task Force**
2320 17th Street NW
Washington, DC 20009-2702
202-332-6483
www.ngltf.org

**National Mental Health Association**
1021 Prince St
Alexandria, VA 22314
800-969-6642
www.nmha.org

**National Organization for Victim Assistance (NOVA)**
757 Park Rd NW
Washington, DC 20010
800-TRY-NOVA
www.access.digex.net/nova

**National Victims Resource Center**
2111 Wilson Blvd., Suite 300
Arlington, VA 22201
800-FYI-CALL
www.nvc.org

**National Center for Missing and Exploited Children**
2101 Wilson Boulevard, Suite 550
Arlington, VA 22201
800-843-5678
www.missingkids.com

**Rape, Abuse, and Incest National Network (RAINN)**
635-B Pennsylvania Ave. SE
Washington, DC 20003
202-544-1034
HOTLINE 800-656-HOPE
www.rainn.org

# Suggested Readings

Anderson, C. "Males as Sexual-Assault Victims: Multiple Levels of Trauma," *Journal of Homosexuality*, 7/2-3 (Winter/Spring 1982).

Aprile, D. "Out of the Shadows," *Courier-Journal,* Louisville, Ky., September 16, 1990.

Bolton, F., L. Morris, and A. MacEachron. *Males at Risk.* Beverly Hills: Sage Publications, 1989.

Braen, G. R. "The Male Rape Victim: Examination and Management," *Rape and Sexual Assault: Management and Intervention.* Germantown, Md.: Aspen Publications, 1980.

Brown, C. *First Get Mad Then Get Justice.* New York: Birch Lane Press, 1993.

Bureau of Justice Statistics. *Sex Offenses and Offenders,* February 1997.

Burgess, A. *The Sexual Victimization of Adolescents.* DHHS Pub. No. (ADM) 85-1382. Rockville, Md.: National Center for the Prevention and Control of Rape, 1985.

Burgess, A., and L. Holmstrom. *Rape Crisis and Recovery.* Bowie, Md.: Robert J. Brady Co., 1979.

Burgess, A., W. Fehder, and C. Harman. "Delayed Reporting of the Rape Victim," *Journal of Psychosocial Nursing* 33/9 (1995).

Burkhart, B., and M. Fromuth. "The Victim: Issues in Identification and Treatment." In T. Jackson (ed.), *Acquaintance Rape: Assessment, Treatment, and Prevention.* Sarasota, Fla.: Professional Resource Press (1996): 145-76.

Butler, S. *Conspiracy of Silence.* Volcano, Calif.: Volcano Press, 1978.

Calderwood, D. "The Male Rape Victim," *Medical Aspects of Human Sexuality* (May 1987).

Clark, D. *Loving Someone Gay*. New York: New American Library, 1977.

Davis, H. C. *Behind and Beyond the Walls: Collection of Essays*. Taft, Okla.: Eddie Warrior Correctional Center, 1997.

Donaldson, S. *Rape of Incarcerated Males in the USA: A Preliminary Statistical Look,* 5th ed., 1994.

Dumond, R. "The Sexual Assault of Male Inmates in Incarcerated Settings," *International Journal of the Sociology of Law* 20 (1992).

Dutton, D. *The Batterer: A Psychological Profile*. New York: Basic Books, 1995.

Epstein, J., and S. Langenbahn. *The Criminal Justice and Community Response to Rape*. Washington, D.C.: U. S. Department of Justice, National Institute of Justice, May 1994.

Estrich, S. *Real Rape*. Cambridge, Mass.: Harvard University Press, 1987.

Fairstein, L. *Sexual Violence*. New York: William Morrow and Co., 1993.

Getlin, J. "Prison Rape Prevalent But Sympathy Hard to Find," *Wichita Eagle*, May 22, 1994.

Groth, N. *Men Who Rape*. New York: Plenum Press, 1979.

Groth, N., and A. W. Burgess. "Male Rape: Offenders and Victims," *American Journal of Psychiatry* 137 (1980).

Hawkins, R., and G. Alpert. *American Prison Systems: Punishments and Justice*. N.J.: Prentice Hall, 1989.

Hiken, L. "Imprisonment—America's Drug of Choice," *Guild Practitioner* 52/3 (1995).

Hunter, M. *Abused Boys*. New York: Ballantine Books, 1990.

James, B. *Treating Traumatized Children*. New York: The Free Press, 1989.

Katherine, A. *Boundaries: Where You End and I Begin*. New York: Parkside Publishing Co., 1991.

Kaufman, A., P. Divasto, and R. Jackson. "Male Rape Victims: Non-Institutionalized Assault," *American Journal of Psychiatry*, 137/2 (February 1980).

Ledray, L. E. *Recovering From Rape*. New York: Henry Holt and Co., 1986.

MacDonald, J. *Rape: Controversial Issues*. Springfield, Ill.: Charles C. Thomas Publisher, 1995.

Matsakis, A. *I Can't Get Over It*. Oakland, Calif.: New Harbinger Publications, 1992.

McEvoy, A., and J. Brookings. *If She is Raped: A Guidebook for Husbands, Fathers, and Male Friends,* 3rd ed. Holmes Beach, Fla.: Learning Publications, 1999.

Mendel, M. P. *The Male Survivor*. Beverly Hills: Sage Publications, 1995.

Mitchell, J., and G. Everly. *Critical Incident Management: A Basic Course Workbook*. Ellicott City, Md.: International Critical Incident Stress Foundation, 1996.

Pharr, S. *Homophobia: A Weapon of Sexism*. Berkeley: Chardon Press, 1997.

Rideau, W., and R. Wilberg. *Rage and Survival Behind Bars*. New York: Times Books, 1992.

Ryan, G., and S. Lane. *Juvenile Sexual Offending*. San Francisco: Jossey-Bass Publishers, 1997.

Salter, A. *Treating Child Sex Offenders and Victims*. Beverly Hills: Sage Publications, 1988.

Scarce, M. *Male on Male Rape*. New York: Insight Books, 1997.

Schudson, C. *On Trial*. Boston: Beacon Press, 1989.

Schwartz, M., and W. DeKeseredy. *Sexual Assault on the College Campus: The Role of Male Peer Support.* Thousand Oaks, Calif.: Sage Publications, 1997.

Selkin, J. *The Child Sexual Abuse Case in the Courtroom.* Denver: Author, 1991.

Sennott, C. "Prison System Enacts Reforms to Stop Inmate Rape," *Boston Globe,* November 9, 1994.

Skinner, C. *Prison Rape Legislation.* Illinois House Bill 2122, February 16, 1995.

Smith, M. *No Longer a Victim.* Tulsa, Okla.: Pillar Books and Publishing, 1992.

Smith, M. "Stigma of Male Rape Hinders Victims' Healing," *Tulsa World,* January 26, 1997.

Stuart, I., and J. Greer. *Victims of Sexual Aggression.* New York: Van Nostrand Reinhold Co., 1984.

Struckman-Johnson, C. "Sexual Coercion Reported by Men and Women in Prison," *The Journal of Sex Research* 33/1 (1996).

Timilty, J. *Prison Journal.* Boston: Northeastern University Press, 1997.

U. S. Department of Justice, Federal Bureau of Prisons. *Sexual Assault Prevention/Intervention Programs.* No. 5324.02, February 2, 1995.

Warshaw, R. *I Never Called It Rape.* New York: Ms. Foundation for Education and Communication, 1988.

Whitcomb, D. *When the Victim is a Child.* Washington, D.C.: U. S. Department of Justice, March 1992.

Zaphiris, A. "The Sexually-Abused Boy," *Preventing Sexual Abuse* (1986).